TRANSRACIAL ADOPTION

TRANSRACIAL
ADOPTION

Rita James Simon
University of Illinois

Howard Altstein
University of Maryland

A Wiley-Interscience Publication

JOHN WILEY & SONS

NEW YORK ■ LONDON ■ SYDNEY ■ TORONTO

Copyright © 1977 by John Wiley & Sons, Inc.

All rights reserved. Published simultaneously in Canada.

Library of Congress Cataloging in Publication Data:

Simon, Rita James.
  Transracial adoption.

  "A Wiley-Interscience publication."
  Includes index.
  1. Interracial adoptions—United States. 2. Afro-Americans—Race identity. 3. Afro-American children. 4. Indians of North American—Race identity. 5. Indians of North America—Children. 6. Oriental children. I. Altstein, Howard, joint author. II. Title.
HV875.S56   362.7'34   76-44817
ISBN 0-471-79208-X

Printed in the United States of America

10 9 8 7 6 5 4 3 2 1

To Julian, David, Judith, and Daniel

□ ■ □ ■

To Helene, Samuel, and Rachel

PREFACE

We started collecting information for this book in 1972. At that time, the transracial adoption of American black and Indian children and of children from South East Asia by white families had been contributing significantly to the removal of "hard to place children" from public institutions into permanent family settings. By the time we finished writing in 1976, transracial adoption had almost disappeared. Its demise was not due to natural causes. Neither the supply of children, nor the availability of potential parents, had been exhausted. Transracial adoption came to a halt largely as a result of the organized efforts of black and Indian leaders who saw in the practice a threat to the future of their communities and to its most valuable resource: their children. Leaders and professional members of these communities viewed adoption of black and Indian children by white parents as acts of cultural genocide. Through the organized efforts of black social workers and Indian council members pressure was brought to bear on family and child care departments in many states with the result that transracial adoption is no longer permitted.

The information contained in this book will not provide all the answers necessary to determine whether transracial adoption has done more good than harm to the children who have been placed in those homes, to the families involved, and to the racial and ethnic communities from which the children were obtained. Such evidence must await later studies, perhaps, fifteen years from now, when the adopted children are adults and the choices as to who they are and to which community they belong have been established. Rather, what we have tried to do in this book is to provide a sensitive, informed discussion of all the issues involved, and of the implications of decisions and rules currently enacted that effect the destiny of these children. We also provide empirical data on the adjustments of the non-white adopted children to their new family, on the quality of the relationships among white and nonwhite children in those families, and on how the children's racial preferences, awarenesses, and identities have been affected by unusual family composition.

The data that served as the basis for information in Chapters 4 and 6 were collected with funds provided by a National Institute of Mental Health Grant (MH 20725). Graduate students who served as interviewers on that study were Margaret Bobertz, Richard de Liberty, Gail Thoen, Brian Sosdian, Susan Smith, and Pamela Wolens. Mary Garrity assisted in the library research. We thank them again for their participation. Special thanks are owed to Carol Sosdian and Michele Long for their assistance in the analysis of the data. Julian Simon and Helene Altstein read early versions of several chapters and their criticisms helped improve them. Frances Baily, Jo Hulett, Sandra Hamilton, Sylvia Farhi were most helpful in typing the manuscript and Carole Appel helped in the editing.

But we owe our biggest debt of gratitude to the families who welcomed us into their homes; to the parents who allowed us to interview them and their children. They gave of their time and their thoughts generously and cordially. We hope we have been successful in accurately portraying their experiences.

RITA JAMES SIMON
HOWARD ALTSTEIN

Urbana-Champaign, Illinois
Baltimore, Maryland
September 1976

CONTENTS

INTRODUCTION

The material in this volume provides three types of information. The first part describes the history, prevalance, and types of transracial adoption in the United States. The beginnings of transracial adoption are traced to the end of World War II and the presence of thousands of homeless children in Europe and Asia. Statistics show transracial adoption on a large scale did not get under way until the mid-1960s, when it was accompanied by major changes in social work and adoption agency policy concerning appropriate criteria for determining which children should be made available to which types of parents.

Indeed, it was not until social workers and adoption agency personnel were able to set aside their convictions about the importance of "matching" potential parents and children that transracial adoption could develop on a large scale. So long as adoption agencies held to the policy that blond, blue-eyed, white-skinned children could be adopted only by parents of similar appearance and background, and that Catholics must adopt Catholics, and Jews, Jews, there was little likelihood that many of the children in need of homes would ever leave the public institutions in which they were being cared for. Even though there are ample data to support the observation that black couples are just as likely to adopt as white families, the number of black children available for adoption far exceeded the supply of prospective black parents. This fact, along with the scarcity of white children, was a major reason why the matching criterion was discarded and the door opened to transracial adoption.

In the United States, two categories of children were most affected by this practice: blacks and Indians. Overseas, Europe was the major source of children following World War II, then Korea, and most recently South Vietnam. At the time of writing, it is estimated that about 15,000 children have been transracially adopted since 1961.

Organized opposition to transracial adoption began in the early part of the 1970s, and by 1975 was formidable enough to bring about a reversal in policy on the part of major adoption agencies in various states throughout the country. The opposition was led and organized primarily by black social workers and leaders of black political organizations who saw in the practice an insidious scheme for depriving the black community of its most valuable future resource: its children. In essence, the leaders of black and Indian organizations argue that non-white children who are adopted by white parents are lost to the non-white community. The experience of growing up in a white world makes it impossible for them to ever take their rightful place among the non-white communities. And this they see as a double tragedy.

On the one hand, the ranks of the black community are being depleted, and those of the white community are growing at the expense of the former. And on the other hand, those black children who cannot "pass into" the white community, because their skin is too dark or their characteristics too distinctively negroid, are cast adrift. They will be blacks with "white psyches," black on the outside and white on the inside, and it will be their lot to stand apart from both communities.

Some of the leaders of American Indian groups labeled transracial adoption "genocide" and accused white society of perpetuating its most malevolent scheme, that of seeking to deny the Indians their future by taking away their children.

Both the blacks and the Indians who led and organized the opposition to transracial adoption agreed on one major point—that it is impossible for white parents to rear black or Indian children in such an environment as to permit them to retain or develop a black or Indian identity. Even if some white parents might wish to do this—and want their adopted children to grow up Indian or black—they lack the skills, insights, and experience necessary for accomplishing such a task. Most of the opposition did not share such positive views. They saw in transracial adoption a diabolical scheme whereby thousands of black and Indian children eventually would pass into the white community.

To a large extent these arguments proved effective in bringing to a halt or greatly reducing the number of transracial adoptions. But it left unsolved the problem that gave rise to the practice in the first place, namely, the presence of large numbers of nonwhite children in public institutions. Solutions other than transracial adoption have since been introduced for meeting this problem.

The third and last section considers the current status of the two most popular innovations: subsidized and single-parent adoptions. Of the two, subsidized adoption enjoys broader support and is more widespread. Its appeal is primarily to black couples who want to adopt one or more children (usually to add to those they already have) and who meet all the criteria for adoption except the financial ones. The presence of a financial subsidy is not intended to limit or change the legal status of the child vis-à-vis his or her adopted parents, and the child is as legally and completely adopted as if there were no subsidy. The primary participants in subsidized adoption programs are black children and black parents.

Not so widespread, and more controversial, is the other innovation that also developed as part of the antitransracial adoption movement: the practice whereby single adults (those who have never been married, as well as those who are widowed or divorced) may legally adopt nonrelated children. As in subsidized adoption programs, blacks are the main participants in single-parent adoptions. While men are not legally excluded from such programs, and there are instances in which the single adopting parent is a male, the program is primarily directed at and mainly involves women.

Section two of this volume describes the results of a survey of about 200 white families who adopted nonwhite children. The major thrust of the study was to find out about the racial identity and racial attitudes of the adopted children as well as their siblings. It also attempted to determine how and what the parents were doing to develop their children's racial awareness and identity. The procedures for assessing the children's attitudes were projective devices similar to those that have been employed by social scientists over the past three and a half decades.

In addition to interviewing the children, field workers solicited the opinions and attitudes of the parents in considerable detail. Not only were the parents asked about their perceptions of the racial identity and attitudes of their children, but also about their own motivation for adopting nonwhite children, their perception of how the adoption has affected the internal dynamics of their family, and their guesses about the future identity of their children and the problems they are likely to confront.

The survey also yielded demographic information about the types of people who adopted transracially, their experiences with social workers and adoption agencies, and the changes the adoption has made in their social roles and status and in the social groups to which they belong.

But unlike other studies involving adopted children, the major thrust of this one was not to assess the successfulness of the adoption per se. This study is not another addition to the library of studies that have sought to measure the extent to which the adopted child (in either a traditional or transracial adoption situation) has adjusted to his or her parents and how the parents feel about their new child and their new role. The major purpose of the survey was to find out how racial attitudes, awareness, and identity were or were not likely to be affected by the merging of different races within a nuclear family. The focus was on the children, not the parents. For that reason we purposely selected young children whose opinions, attitudes, and perceptions on these matters were still in the formative stage.

When the field work for the survey began in 1971, transracial adoption was a much publicized, rather extensively used procedure for removing nonwhite children from institutions and placing them in nuclear family settings. It continued to gain momentum for a few more years. But the opposition to it and the attacks on it developed at an ever faster rate, and the intensity of feelings against the practice was no match for the ambivalence most social workers and adoption agencies had felt about transracial adoption from the outset. The leading and most enthusiastic supporters of transracial adoption were parents who had adopted transracially. The organizations they founded, such as the Open Door Society and the Council on Adoptable Children mounted counteroffensives, but they were not effective enough to turn the tide. By the time this book was written transracial adoptions of American black and Indian children by white parents were just about over. If some such placements are still being made, the numbers are so small as to be insignificant.

Chapters 4 and 6 describe what happened in families when the adopted children were less than 8 years old and when they had been in their adoptive home for a few years. It will remain for time, and perhaps a later study about 15 years hence, to find out how things really worked out—to find out who these children are racially and socially, what racial attitudes they hold, how they feel about what has happened to them, with which racial communities and social groups they affiliate, and to which community they want their own children to belong.

These and other questions that only time, and a future study, can answer are whether families such as those surveyed in this study will have produced individuals who are "color blind" and whether these individuals will serve as the nucleus for a new community that does not perceive social differences on the basis of race and which does not identify individuals in traditional racial categories.

In the meantime, this volume will describe the nature of such issues and emotions in American society in 1976.

SECTION ONE

BACKGROUND AND REVIEW
OF EARLY WORK

This section provides a brief history of transracial adoption, an accounting of the numbers and types of children who have been involved, and a review of the opposition that has developed. In so doing, it sets the stage for the description and interpretation of Section Two. An important theme which runs throughout this volume, but is stated most prominently in this section, is the rise, development, expansion, and eventual demise of the transracial adoption movement. This section also comments on the various ideologies surrounding adoption, which made transracial adoptions difficult, then aided in its success, and at the time of writing are contributing to its demise.

Chapters 2 and 3 review prior empirical studies of families who adopted American black or Indian children and report the major finding of these studies. The circumstances surrounding the most recent instance of intercountry transracial adoptions are documented in detail in Chapter 3, where Vietnamese adoptions are considered. This first section may be viewed as a prologue to the discussion of the empirical findings obtained in the survey described in Section Two.

CHAPTER ONE

TRANSRACIAL ADOPTION: HISTORY, PREVALENCE, AND LEGAL STATUS

Adoption has existed since the pharaoh's daughter found Moses among the reeds of the Nile. But the idea has also persisted throughout history that to be adopted is somehow to be different, deviant. In fact, as recently as the early 1920s the "hard-to-place" child was almost every child needing a home, including "blue-ribbon" infants (white, healthy, Protestant).[1]

The history of adoption is the history of hard-to-place children. In the case of transracial adoption the children are nonwhite and the adoptive parents are white. The hard-to-place concept of the nonwhite child is not unlike the overall position of nonwhites in our society—hard to place educationally, socially, and politically. One of the reasons for the ardent support as well as

9

the antagonism that has surrounded transracial adoption almost from its inception is that, in addition to any adoptive child being viewed as somehow deviant, it represents the other side of the traditional matching coin.

Adoption agencies historically have attempted to equate a child's individual characteristics with those of the intended adoptive parents. Not only were similar physical and at times intellectual qualities seen as important components in adoptive criteria, but identical religious backgrounds were defined, at times by law, as essential.[2] Thus the battle of transreligious adoption preceded the movement toward transracial adoption, and it was not until the conceptual and pragmatic acceptance of transreligious adoption occurred that transracial adoption could and did develop.

As adoption moved toward becoming an acceptable means to deal with children who need parents and couples who want children, so too social work evolved into a recognized discipline. This relationship was not coincidental. Adoption agencies are a relatively new phenomenon. Historically, most adoptions resulted from negotiations between attorneys for potential adoptive parents, a private physician whose patient wanted to surrender a child, or an orphanage. The natural parent's rights would be waived, and the court would usually grant the adoption petition. A gap existed, however, between a couple's desire to adopt and the courts' ability to determine whether or not the petitioners would indeed be adequate parents.

Social work, or what was to develop into social work, sought to fill this gap by being the advocate for both couples wanting to adopt and women or institutions wanting to surrender children. Beginning, as they traditionally did in most spheres of social welfare, as volunteers, social workers gradually "professionalized" the adoptive process. In its successful bid to establish organizational legitimacy, social work has profoundly influenced the growth of transracial adoption and has been closely identified with the matching concept. This influence is a practical result of a long-standing involvement with the field of adoption. Since the beginning of the twentieth century, law, medicine, and the legislative and judicial branches of government have traditionally turned to social work for help in what has matured into an advise-and-consent union. The development of transracial adoption, then, is linked to social work's attitude toward it.

Transracial adoption began in the late 1940s. It gained momentum in the mid-1950s. It diminished during the early 1960s, rose again in the mid-1960s, and waned in the early 1970s. At the time of writing (1975), transracial adoption has almost ceased to exist. For example, of the 4665 black children adopted in 1973 by unrelated petitioners, only 1091 were placed with white families. The latter figure represents a 30 percent decrease from 1972.[3] The closeness of these stages to international developments (e.g., World War II, the Korean and Vietnam wars) is not accidental, nor is the position of transracial adoption accidental to the overall relationship between white and nonwhite communities in the United States since the early 1950s. Most of the social forces that define white-nonwhite relationships are evident in the development of transracial adoption, from white paternalism, through the civil rights movement, and culminating in a militant awareness of nonwhite racial minorities of their social, economic, and political influence.

The development of transracial adoption was not a result of deliberate agency programming to serve populations in need, but rather an accommodation to reality. Recent social changes regarding abortion, contraception, and reproduction in general had significantly reduced the number of white children available for adoption, leaving nonwhite children as the largest available source.[4] Changes had also occurred regarding the willingness of white couples to adopt nonwhite children.

Given these social changes, adoptive parents may have considered transracial adoption the most effective way of dealing with their childlessness, or as a humanitarian gesture to expiate for some individual or collective guilt vis-à-vis race relations. Whatever the reasons, in order to remain "in business," adoption agencies were forced by a combination of social conditions to reevaluate their ideology, traditionally geared toward the matching concept, in order to serve in tandem the joint needs of these two groups.

In the United States the groups initially involved in adoption across racial lines seem quite clearly to have been motivated by humanitarian principles and a sense of social responsibility. Significantly, their efforts beginning in the late 1940s were directed toward adopting children from outside the United States. Intercountry adoptions preceded the development of intracountry transracial adoption. The arguments in favor of intercountry adoptions are essentially similar to those later used in support of transracial adoption, namely, that is better for both children and adoptive parents if the former are raised in a family situation than if they remain either in an institution or in foster care.[5] Opponents of intercountry adoptions argue just as vehemently that to transplant a child from his or her own culture is to court possible future personal confusion and societal rejection.

Large-scale intercountry adoption began shortly after World War II and initially involved children from Germany, Estonia, and Latvia brought to this country through the efforts of Lutheran social service agencies. During the period 1948–1957, especially beginning with the Refugee Relief Act of 1953 (repealed in 1961), which allowed a visa to be granted for a child · adopted by proxy, 772 immigrant children were adopted by American families, of whom 206 children were Asian, mainly from Japan and Korea.[6]

In 1953, the Seventh Day Adventists started placing Korean children with American families.[7] They were followed by the Catholic Relief Service and Harry Holt, founder of the Holt Adoption Program, Inc.[8] The year 1953 predates by several years the transracial adoption of native-born nonwhite children in meaningful numbers.[9]

By June 1974, of the 4770 immigrant children admitted into the United States for purposes of adoption, 75 percent were Asian, and 68 percent of these were Korean. Most of the latter were admitted under the auspices of the Holt Adoption Program. Vietnamese children accounted for only 16 percent of the Asian children, but these figures predate the events of March–April, 1975, when thousands of Vietnamese children were airlifted into the country (see Chapter 3). Of the remaining children, 10 percent were admitted from North America, 7 percent from Europe and Latin America, and 1 percent from Africa and Oceania.[10]

Available data indicate that, from June 1961 to June 1974, 33,237 immigrant children were admitted into the United States, of whom 21,635 (65 percent) were defined as nonwhite (Asian, African, South American).[11] A reasonable assumption is that most nonwhite children entered this country for the purpose of transracial adoption, although this is not expressly indicated in the data's source. In fact, when the figures for June 1961–June 1974 are compared with the 1974 estimated total number of 15,000 transracially adopted children, there appears to be a discrepancy of approximately 6600. Perhaps this can be explained by suggesting that these children are either in foster care or institutions. In other words, that they are awaiting adoption in nonfamilial placements.

THE MATCHING CONCEPT

Perhaps the most profound effect transracial adoption has had on the field of adoption has been that it has reduced the field's historic reliance on the concept of matching. The idea that child and adoptive parents were to be matched remained almost inviolate until the advent of intercountry adoption: "A child wants to be like his parents . . . parents can more easily identify with a child who resembles them . . . the fact of adoption should not be. accentuated by placing a child with parents who are different from him."[12]

The assumptions of matching are simple, but naive. In order to ensure against adoptive failure, adoption agencies felt that both the adopted child and his or her potential parents should be matched quite literally on as many physical, emotional, and cultural characteristics as possible. The most important were racial and religious characteristics.

Thus it was not uncommon for potential adoptive parents to be denied a child if their hair and eye color could not be duplicated in an adoptable child. The hypothesis of matching was one of equalization. If all possible physical, emotional, intellectual, racial, and religious differences between adoptor and child could be reduced hopefully to zero, the relationship stood a better chance of succeeding. So ingrained was the matching idea, that its assumptions, especially those relating to religion and race, were operationalized into law under the rubric of a "child's best interests." Seventeen states, including the District of Columbia, had at one time or another, or presently have, statutes pertaining to the religious matching of adopted children and parents.[13]

In 1954 a study was made which requested adoption agencies to indicate whether certain factors were significant for evaluating the possibilities of placing a child with a particular family. Table 1.1 summarizes the agencies' responses.[14]

While there appears to be wide variation in the matching factors considered important by the individual agencies, all the characteristics mentioned on the checklist were defined as important by at least two-thirds of the agencies. Only 10 agencies felt that it was not important to equate a child's race to that of his prospective parent. Shapiro, the author of the study, commented,

We know from practice that agencies are not placing Negro children in white homes or white children in Negro homes. Some agencies use homes for children of mixed racial background where the background of the adoptive parents is not the same as the child's. However, in most instances the characteristics of the child are primarily white, for this kind of placement occurs more frequently with children of mixed Oriental or Indian and white background, than with children in whom the non-Caucasian blood is Negro.[15]

In its *Standards for Adoption Service* (SAS) the Child Welfare League of America (CWLA), continued to make matching a responsible part of adoption practice. Under the subtitle "Matching," the CWLA in 1959, recom-

TABLE 1.1 Matching factors adoption agencies considered important

Matching Factors	Important		Total Number of Responses
	Yes	No	
Level of intelligence and intellectual potential	253	1	254
Religious background	240	13	253
Racial background	240	10	250
Temperamental needs	235	12	247
Educational background	204	41	245
Physical resemblance to child	212	30	242
Geographic separation from natural parents	192	49	241
Cultural background	195	40	235
Nationality background	163	69	232
Physical characteristics of child's family	187	42	229

Source: Michael Shapiro, A Study of Adoption Practice: Adoption

Agencies and the Children They Serve, vol. 1 (Child Welfare

League of America, New York, April, 1956), p. 84, Table 7,

Basis for Matching.

mended that "similarities of background or characteristics should not be a major consideraion in the selection of a family, except where integration of the child into the family and his identification with them may be facilitated by likeness, as in the case of some older children or some children with distinctive physical traits, such as race." When the age of the child and of the adoptive parents were considered, the SAS suggested that "the parents selected for a child should be within the age range usual for natural parents of a child of that age."[16]

Recognizing that social and cultural attitudes are learned rather than inherited, the SAS did not recommend that these factors enter into the matching equation. The educational background of both the child's biological family and the prospective adoptive parents were likewise minimized: "The home selected should be one in which the child will have the opportunity to develop his own capacities, and where he is not forced to meet unrealistic expectations of the adoptive parents."[17]

Religion was handled in the 1959 SAS by including a rather lengthy statement representing the positions of the three major faiths:

Opportunity for religious and spiritual development of the child is essential in an adoptive home. A child should ordinarily be placed in a home where the religion of adoptive parents is the same as that of the child, unless the parents have specified that the child should or may be placed with a family of another religion. Every effort (including interagency and interstate referrals) should be made to place the child within his own faith, or that designated by his parents. If however, such matching means that placement might never be feasible, or involves a substantial delay in placement, or placement in a less suitable home, a child's need for a permanent family of his own requires that consideration should then be given to placing the child in a home of a different religion. For children whose religion is not known, and whose parents are not accessible, the most suitable home available should be selected.[18]

When dealing with physical characteristics, the SAS reiterated the overall stance toward racial matching and defined the latter as a "physical characteristic": "Physical resemblances should not be a determining factor in the selection of a home, with the possible exception of such racial characteristics as color."[19]

By 1964 the matching concept underwent a subtle but significant shift. In a CWLA publication written by Viola M. Bernard, the following statement appeared:

In the past much emphasis was placed on similarities, especially of physical appearance, as well as national, sociocultural, and ethnic backgrounds. It was thought, for example, that matching the child's hair color, physique and complexion to that of the adoptive parents would facilitate the desired emotional identification between them. Experience has shown, however, that couples can identify with children whose appearance and background differ markedly from their own. Instead, optimal "matching" nowadays puts more stress on other kinds of correspondencies between the child's *estimated potentialities* and the parents' personalities, values, and modes of life. Respective temperaments, for example, are taken into account. Whether similarities or differences work out better depends on many factors, which also must be considered.

Although it has been proven repeatedly that parents can identify with children of different emotional and racial backgrounds, and with all sorts of heredities, not every couple, of course, feels equally accepting of each type of "difference." Accordingly, the child of a schizophrenic parent would not be considered for a couple who has deeply rooted fears about the inheritance of mental illness; a child of interracial background who appears predominately white is likely to adjust best in a white family. [Emphasis added.][20]

What seems to have occurred in 1964 is a redefinition of matching. No longer were the most ostensible characteristics to be matched between child and parent. Instead, emphasis was to be placed on a child's "estimated potentialities." In other words, the "unseen" instead of the "seen," were to be matched except with regard to race. Racial matching, however, continued to be stressed by the CWLA, as indicated by the following statement. "A child who appears predominately white will ordinarily adjust best in a white family."[21]

In 1968, the subtitle "Matching" was deleted from the CWLA's SAS. In its stead there appeared a category entitled, "Responsibility for Selection of Family." Its wording was broad and somewhat ambiguous vis-à-vis matching but quite clear about the role of the professional social worker and the adoption agency: "The professional social work staff of the agency (including the social worker who knows the child, the social worker who knows the adoptive family and the supervisor) should carry the responsibility for the selection of a family for a particular child on the basis of their combined knowledge about both the child and the adoptive family and the findings and recommendations of all the consultants."[22]

Age as a matching criterion was expanded past its 1958 statement and, as a result, it became less potent as a critical matching factor: "The parents selected for a child should be ones who are likely to retain the capacities needed to adapt to the changing needs of a child as he grows up."[23]

The social, cultural, and national background of either the child or the adoptive parents was treated in a manner similar to the 1959 SAS treatment. Educational background was likewise generally reflective of the 1959 statement.

Two important rewordings appeared within the categories "Religion" and "Physical and Personality Characteristics." Absent from the "Religion" category was the lengthy statement in the 1959 description that related to the rationale for religious matching. What appeared instead was the following. "The family selected for a child should be one in which the child will have an opportunity for religious or spiritual and ethical development but religious background alone should not be the basis for selection of a family for a child."[24]

In 1975, however, a New York State court upheld the practice of placing children along religious lines. The court found no constitutional inconsistency with the provisions of the law which stated that "so far as consistent with the best interests of the child and where practicable" a child should be placed with an agency that reflected the child's religious faith.[25]

Since most blacks are Protestant and the number of homeless black children far exceeds the capability of Protestant agencies to care for them adequately, a situation now exists in New York whereby these children, for lack of other alternatives, are placed in state agencies.

Absent from the category "Physical and Personality Characteristics" was any reference to color as a criterion for adoption. Color was originally defined as a physical characteristic. What appeared was a rather definitive statement which precluded the possibility that either physical or personality traits would be considered determinants of adoption: "Physical resemblances of the adoptive parents, the child or his natural parents, should not be a determining factor in the selection of a home."[26]

By 1971, then, most of the characteristics traditionally encompassed within the matching concept appeared to have been reworded to the point of being broad guidelines rather than precise definitions. Witness the following statement from the CWLA's *Guidelines for Adoption Service* (not to be confused with the SAS).

When adoption has been found desirable for the child, and the couple has met the agency's requirements for adoption, an appraisal must be made of their suitability for each other. In most instances, similarity in background or characteristics need not be a factor. It should be recognized, however, that people vary in their capacity to accept differences. If the couple want a child who is like them in certain ways, this desire should be taken into consideratio· [27]

Finally, all the major categories mentioned in previous editions of the SAS remain intact in the most recent edition. Matching thus continues to be a classic principle of adoption practice, although it has been significantly diluted.

THE LEGAL STATUS OF TRANSRACIAL ADOPTION

In theory, the authority to approve petitions for any type of adoption is judicial power. In practice, power is exercised by the social work profession in the name of the adoption agency. Historically, the courts have recognized that they do not possess the requisite evaluative expertise and have relegated to social work the task of determining whether potential adoptive parents are fit to serve in that capacity, but they have retained their (seldom used) prerogative to deny an agency's recommendation.[28] Thus, in most cases, it was the quality of social work's assessment of what was deemed to be in a child's best interests, as recommended to and interpreted by the court, that marked the legal status of adoption, specifically of transracial adoption. The court's position was one of response rather than initiation.

Adoption, or the legal formation of a parent-child union, unknown in common law, was initially permitted by statute in the United States by means of a deed without benefit of any judicial procedure. At first it was approved only in those states whose legal system was based on civil law, and it was not until 1851, when a Massachusetts statute was passed, that a requirement for a formal court hearing was introduced. The Massachusetts law is usually credited with being the first adoption statute. By 1931, every state had adoption laws, with some variation as to their emphasis.[29] However, the overriding concern of most adoption laws is a judicial rendering of whether a child's best interests will be served by granting an adoption petition. The fact that 41 states plus the District of Columbia use this concept (a child's best interests) attests to its significance.[30] In addition, both Australia and New Zealand also stress this concept.[31]

Race as a variable in adoption proceedings has been dealt with in several ways. Up until recently Texas and Louisiana denied adoption petitions across racial lines. The statutes of both states were declared unconstitutional in 1967 and 1972, respectively.[32] As of 1971, however, as can be seen by the wording of South Carolina's adoption law, black parents were not able to adopt white children, but white parents were permitted to adopt black children:

It shall be unlawful for any parent, relative, or other white person in this State, having the control or custody of any white child by right to guardianship, natural or acquired or otherwise, to dispose of, give or surrender such white child permanently into the custody, control maintenance or support of a Negro. Any person violating the provisions of this section shall be guilty of a misdemeanor. The provisions of this section shall not be construed so as to prevent the offices of a Negro in the family of any white person as a nurse.[33]

Other states mention race as an important factor in granting adoption (e.g., Georgia, New Hampshire, Ohio),[34] but most make no reference to it at all. In any event, as previously noted, the final decision is made by the judge's interpretation of the best interests of the child, allowing for the inevitable judicial inconsistencies not unlike discretionary decisions made by social agencies involved in the investigation and approval of potential adoptive parents.

One of the first and most important cases concerning transracial adoption involved a 1955 decision by the Washington, D.C., Court of Appeals.[35] In 1949, an out-of-wedlock child was born to a white woman. The putative father was also white. In 1951, the woman married a black man who, with the mother's permission, petitioned to adopt her son. The whereabouts of the boy's putative father were unknown. Even though the child had continually lived with his mother and her husband, the district court denied the adoption petition, stating: "This situation gives rise to a difficult social problem. The boy when he grows up might lose the social status of a white man by reason of the fact that by his record his father will be a Negro. I feel the court should not fashion the child's future in this manner."[36] The district court's decision was overruled by the appellate court on the ground that the court's primary function was to evaluate what was best for the child and that denial of the petition could not be based "on a distinction between the 'social status' of whites and Negroes."[37] It seemed apparent that the element of race was not to be the sole consideration in determining a child's future, thereby depriving him of a legitimate status.

Two additional cases seven years later shed some further light on judicial thinking regarding transracial adoption. In 1962, the probate court in Cleveland, Ohio, denied a petition for adoption because of the racial background of both the intended adoptive parents and the child.[38] The case involved a white male, his naturalized Japanese wife, and a child born out of wedlock of English and Puerto Rican background who had been placed in a social agency. Because of the child's racial combination, the agency found it very difficult to place her in foster care. Eventually, she was placed with the petitioners for adoption, the agency reporting to the court that its investigation revealed the intended adoptive parents to be qualified to assume their roles.

The appellate court felt that only the child's best interests should be decisive in any disposition, especially since the social agency fully endorsed the petitioners to be highly capable, and it ordered the probate court to grant the adoption petition.

That same year a wealthy Long Island, New York, couple with three natural and two adopted children (one Korean and one black) petitioned the Commissioner of Welfare to adopt another black child who was being boarded by the county welfare department at a county-operated geriatric center.[39] When their request was refused, they petitioned the Supreme Court of the county and were likewise denied. Grounds for denial were that they already had five children (i.e., demonstrated fecundity), that they had only recently adopted a child, and that the mother desired to continue her career as a teacher.

In this case the court avoided the question of race, preferring instead to sustain the Department of Welfare's discretionary decision, and cited the 1955 case as precedent.

The three cases just mentioned demonstrate only a tentative direction regarding the court's thinking on transracial adoption. The facts remain that in the 1955 Washington decision the child would, in any event, have continued to live with his natural mother whether the petition for adoption was granted or denied. The first 1962 case in Ohio, although an important ruling, did not pertain to blacks, the race most often involved in transracial adoption. The second 1962 ruling was clearly a blow to transracial adoption and a decision probably not in the best interests of the child.

Thus, until 1974, when the matter was adoption *qua* transracial adoption, the court's record was only suggestive. In 1974, in a case involving a county welfare department, the Ohio Supreme Court ruled in favor of the petitioners.[40] Clearly stating race (i.e., heredity) as one factor in its decision, a county welfare department refused to allow the adoption of a black child by her white foster parents. After hearings in the probate and appeals courts, the Supreme Court ruled in favor of the petitioners.

In matters of custody (the legitimization of interracial families with children) as well, the various individual contingencies appear to weigh heavily on the court's decisions. For example, the court usually rules in favor of a white mother (divorced from her white husband) who marries a black man when custody of a child is challenged by the (maternal) grandparents.[41] But when two white *parents* are involved in litigation for custody of their child, the fact that the mother has married a black has strongly affected the court's decision to have custody remain with the father, denying (all the while) that race has in any way been a factor in its decision.[42]

However, when custody of the children of an interracial couple was given to the black father and on subsequent petition from the mother (now married to a white), was awarded to her, race was also considered not to be a factor in the decision.[43]

In what appears to be a landmark case, the California Supreme Court in 1968 refused to allow race to enter into its judicial deliberations when a white father petitioned to have custody of his two children because his former wife had married a black man.[44] The court ruled that it would be unconstitutional to even consider the stepfather's race a factor in the custody hearing.

In a 1975 case in which race was apparently not considered a relevant factor, a white couple petitioned a Maryland Court of Appeals for permanent custody of a seven-year-old child placed in their charge in 1972 by a Montana Crow Indian tribal court. Three years later at the request of the child's biological Indian mother, the tribal court issued a new order opposing the granting of custody. The white couple then sought to have a local county circuit court issue the needed ruling. The Court of Appeals, however, declared that a county circuit court could not give the couple an order granting custody of the child and unanimously ruled that a state court had no jurisdiction in the case. The appeals judge wrote: "There can be no greater threat to essential tribal relations, and no greater infringement on the right of the Crow tribe to govern themselves than to interfere with tribal control over the custody of their children." In supporting his ruling the justice cited an 1832 Supreme Court decision by Chief Justice John Marshall: "The United States has been a jealous sovereign, denying the states any authority over Indian reservations."[45]

CONCLUDING REMARKS

The Fourteenth Amendment calls for the elimination of all forms of racial discrimination. To have any type of statute infringing on an individual's freedom because of his or her race is therefore unconstitutional. Laws prohibiting transracial adoption fall into this category. Nevertheless, certain fundamental questions remain unanswered. For example, does a child have the right to be adopted, or is it a privilege bestowed on him or her by the courts? And do individuals have the right to adopt, given the availability of children, or, as in the case of a child is it a judicially sanctioned privilege?

The answers to these questions appear to be further clouded when the issue of race is added. Although race may be an important factor in considering transracial adoption, it is not to be the *overriding factor*. The courts, in establishing this concept, have announced a broad guideline. But in the process of operationally defining the phrase "a child's best interest," the discretionary use of both social work and judicial authority in recommending and approving individual transracial adoption still remains.

The current legal status of transracial adoption appears to be in the direction of not considering race the sole basis on which adoption petitions are denied. But in all likelihood cases that are contested will be forced to rely on the discretionary interpretation of the two professions most closely involved with transracial adoption, social work and law.

Unfortunately, neither social work nor the courts appear consistent in either their recommendations or decisions. For example, in June 1973, the director of the Illinois Department of Children's and Family Services, prodded by a group of black social workers within his department, ordered a policy change prohibiting approval of transracial adoptions involving black children. One of the stated rationales for the policy change was the belief that sufficient numbers of black adoptive parents existed in the community, which therefore precluded transracial adoption even as a last resort.[46]

If society's basic concern is for a child's welfare, our social orientation suggests it would be more in the child's best interest to grow up in a family situation than to suffer the often dire effects of long-term institutionalization or, to a lesser degree, the insecurity of foster placement. It is reasonable then for agencies to recommend and the courts to grant legitimate transracial adoption petitions where racial origin is only one component of the entire perspective. For a child to be transracially adopted into an accepting family would mitigate most rational objections based on racial differences.

NOTES

1. Joseph H. Reid, "Ensuring Adoption for Hard-to-Place Children," *Child Welfare*, vol. 35, no. 3 (March 1956), pp. 4–8.
2. Alfred Kadushin, "Child Welfare: Adoption and Foster Care," *Encyclopedia of Social Work*, vol. 103, National Association of Social Workers, New York, 1971, pp. 107–111.
3. *Opportunity: A Division of the Boys and Girls Aid Society of Oregon*, Portland, Oreg., mimeographed, December 2, 1974.
4. Historically, there has always been a much larger number of potential adoptive parents than available healthy adoptable children. See Steven V. Roberts, "Supply of Adoptable White Babies Shrinks," *New York Times*, July 18, 1971, p. 28; and Judith Klemsrud, "Adoption Costs Soar as Births Decline," *New York Times*, February 20, 1973, p. 40.
5. H. M. Skeels, "Effects of Adoption on Children from Institutions," *Children*, vol. 12, no. 1 (January–February, 1965), pp. 33–34; A. Kadushin, "Adoptive Parenthood: A Hazardous Adventure?" *Social Work*, vol. 2, no. 3 (November 1966), pp. 30–39; M. L. Pringle-Kellmer, *Adoption: Facts and Fallacies*, Longmans, London, 1967) H. Witmer, E. Herzog, E. Weinstein, and M. E. Sullivan, *Independent Adoptions: A Follow-Up Study*, Russell Sage Foundation, New York, 1963.
6. Hyung Bok Kim and John E. Adams, "A Fresh Look at Intercountry Adoption" *Children*, vol. 18, no. 6 (November–December 1971), pp. 214–221.

7. See Helen Miller, "Korean International Children," *Lutheran Social Welfare* (Summer 1971), pp. 12–23.

8. Kim and Adams, *op. cit.*, footnote 5.

9. In 1970, only 2284 black children were transracially adopted in the United States as compared with 2409 intercountry adoptions for the same year. The number of transracial adoptions involving black children in 1971 rose to 2574. *Opportunity* (September 19, 1973).

10. *Opportunity* (August 1973); United States Department of Justice, Immigration and Naturalization Service, *Immigrant Orphans Admitted to the United States, by Country or Region of Birth, Year Ended June 30, 1974*, Washington, D.C., 1974.

11. These figures represent the combined annual totals noted in footnote 10.

12. Michael Shapiro, *A Study of Adoption Practice: Adoption Agencies and the Children They Serve*, vol. 1, p. 84, Child Welfare League of America, New York, 1965, quoted in Ruth Taft, "Adoptive Families for 'Unadoptable' Children," *Child Welfare*, vol. 32, no. 6 (June 1953), pp. 5–9.

13. Jacqueline and Stewart Macaulay, "Adoptive Placement of Black Children: A Study of Discretion and Legal Norms," unpublished study, University of Wisconsin Law School, Madison, 1974, footnote 15.

14. Shapiro, *op. cit.*, footnote 12, p. 84, Table 7.

15. *Ibid.*, p. 85.

16. Child Welfare League of America, *Standards for Adoption Service*, Child Welfare League of America, New York, 1959, p. 24.

17. *Ibid.*, p. 26.

18. *Ibid.*, p. 25.

19. *Ibid.*, p. 26.

20. Viola M. Bernard, *Adoption*, Child Welfare League of America, New York, 1964, p. 99. (Emphasis added.)

21. Child Welfare League of America, *op. cit.*, footnote 16.

22. Child Welfare League of America, *Standards for Adoption Service*, revised, Child Welfare League of America, New York, 1968, p. 34.

23. *Ibid.*

24. *Ibid.*, p. 35.

25. "Court Finds No Religious Conflict in Wilder vs Sugarman," *Child Welfare League Newsletter*, vol. 5, no. 1 (Winter 1975).

26. Child Welfare League of America, *op. cit.*, footnote 22, p. 35.

27. Child Welfare League of America, *Guidelines for Adoption Service*, Child Welfare League of America, 1971, p. 13.

28. "Foster Pair May Lose Bright Girl," *New York Times*, March 7, 1960, p. 21; Nan Robertson, "Parents Plead Love in Bright Girl Case," *New York Times*, March 9, 1960, p. 27.

29. Michael Shapiro, *A Study of Adoption Practice*, vol. 16, Child Welfare League of America, New York, 1966, p. 12.

30. Macaulay and Macaulay, *op. cit.*, footnote 13.

31. Eileen Saunders, *A Guide to Adoption in New Zealand*, A. W. Reed, Wellington, New Zealand, 1971.

32. In re Gomez, 424 S.W. 2d 656 (Tex. Civ. App., 1967); Compos v. McKeithen, 341 F. Supp. 264 (E.D. la, 1972).

33. South Carolina Code 10-2587.9 et seq. (Supp. 1972).

34. Georgia Code Ann. 74-411(6) (1973); New Hampshire Rev. Stat. Ann. 461.2 (1968); Ohio Rev. Code 3107.05 (E) (P. 1972).

35. In re Adoption of a Minor, 228 F. 2d 446 (D.C. cir. 1953).

36. *Ibid.,* 228 F. 2d 447.

37. *Ibid.,* 228 F. 2d 448.

38. *Ibid.*

39. Matter of the Adoption of Baker, 117 Hiopp. 26, 185 N.E. 2d 51 (1962).

40. Rockefeller v. Nickerson, 36 Misc. 2d 869, 233 N.Y.S. 2d 314 (Sup. Ct. 1962).

41. People ex. rel. Portnoy v. Strasser, 303 N.Y. 539, 104 N.E. 2d 895 (1952).

42. Stingley v. Wesch, 77 Ill., App. 2d 472, 222 N.E. 2d 505 (1966); Murphy v. Murphy, 143 Conn. 600, 124 A2d 891 (1956).

43. Potter v. Potter, 372 Mich. 637, 127 N.W. 2d, 320 (1964).

44. Fountaine v. Fountaine, 9 Ill. App. 2d 482, 133 N.E. 2d 532 (1956).

45. Edward Coltman, "Vista Pair Loses Child to Indians," *Baltimore Sun,* November 14, 1975, p. C1.

46. "White Adoptions," *Chicago Defender,* July 14, 1973; "Transracial Adoptions," *Decatur Herald,* July 22, 1973; "A Sour Adoption Policy," Louis A. Fitzgerald, Jr., *Chicago Defender,* July 23, 1973, p. 8; "Rep. Corneal Davis Rips Adoption Policy," Simeon B. Osby, *Chicago Defender,* October 8, 1973, p. 4; "Transracial Adoption Ban Is Backward Step," Quida Lindsey, *Chicago Sun Times,* August 5, 1973.

CHAPTER TWO

ADOPTIONS OF BLACK CHILDREN BY WHITE PARENTS

This chapter examines two major issues. It reviews statistics and studies about transracial adoption as it affected American black children, and it summarizes the sources, substance, and effectiveness of the opposition to transracial adoption as it developed in the early part of the 1970s.

The institutionalized beginnings of transracial adoption of American black children are traceable to the activities of the Children's Service Center and a group of parents in Montreal, Quebec, Canada, who in 1960 founded an organization known as the Open Door Society.

In the early 1950s the Children's Service Center sought placement for black children in its care among the Canadian black community.[1] It worked with black community leaders and the mass media in its efforts to find black homes for these children but was unsuccessful. The center then turned to its list of white adoptive parents, and the first transracial adoptions were made. Between 1951 and 1963 five black and 66 biracial children were transracially adopted by white families.

In the United States, 1961 marked the founding of an organization whose original purpose was to provide placements in black adoptive homes for black children. Parents to Adopt Minority Youngsters (PAMY) was founded in Minnesota and worked in cooperation with the Minnesota Department of Public Welfare. PAMY was one of the first groups to be formed in this country along the lines of the Open Door Society in Canada and provided similar referral, recruitment, and public relations functions. But PAMY's involvement with transracial adoption, unlike that of the Open Door Society, came as an unexpected by-product of its original intent which was to secure black adoptive homes for black children. From 1962 through 1965 approximately 20 black children in Minnesota were adopted by white families through the efforts of PAMY. These adoptive parents seemed not to fit the traditional stereotyped model of the adoptive family. They were for the most part not infertile, and their act was not seen by them as a substitute for natural parenthood.[2]

By 1969, 47 organizations similar to the Open Door Society were in existence in the United States (Families for Interracial Adoption, the Council on Adoptable Children, Opportunity, The National Council of Adoptive Parents, and Adopt-A-Child-Today).[3] Their major function was to help secure adoptive homes for all parentless children, with particular emphasis on children with "special needs."

PREVALENCE OF BLACK ADOPTIONS BY WHITE FAMILIES

Historically, both private and public adoption agencies have had a bank of white adoptive families in excess of the number of white children.[4] For example, a 1955 study indicated that at any given time there were between two and eight approved white adoptive homes ·for every white child, whereas there was only one approved black family for every 10 to 20 black children.[5]

As can be seen in Table 2.1, by 1970 the number of available nonwhite children still far exceeded the number of approved nonwhite homes. There were 21,416 approved white homes for 18,392 available white children, and 1584 approved nonwhite homes for 4045 available nonwhite children. This resulted in 2461 nonwhite children being technically without (non-

TABLE 2.1 Approved homes and available children, by race and by agency auspices (240 agencies)

Auspices	Number of Agencies	Race	Approved Homes		Children Available		Difference between No. Homes and Children
			Number	Percentage	Number	Percentage	
Public	73	White	4,960	91	4,239	78	721
		Non-white	511	9	1,162	22	-651
		Total	5,471	100	5,401	100	70
Voluntary	167	White	16,456	94	14,153	83	2,303
		Non-white	1,073	6	2,883	17	-1,810
		Total	17,529	100	17,036	100	493
Total	240	White	21,416	93	18,392	82	3,024
		Non-white	1,584	7	4,045	18	-2,461
		Total	23,000	100	22,437	100	563

Source: Lucille Grow, A New Look at Supply and Demand in Adoption (New York, Child Welfare League of America, 1970), p. 8, Table 4.

white) adoptors. These data are based on a survey by the CWLA to which 240 adoption agencies responded out of the 320 contacted.

Combining the figures for public and private agencies shows that there were 116 approved white homes for every 100 white children, and only 39 approved nonwhite homes per available 100 nonwhite children. The fact that transracial adoption was not considered by the agencies in this survey as a way of reducing the excess of available nonwhite children is demonstrated by the following excerpt: "Again, the reader must be cautioned that the data do not take account of the white adoptive homes that are in fact available for the placement of non-white children. If it were *possible* to place a non-white child in about one out of every nine approved white homes, there would be an available adoption resource for all children reported by the 240 agencies."[6] The implication of this 1970 statement is that it is impossible to consider the placement of nonwhite children with white families.

As can be seen in Table 2.2, the Middle Atlantic region, with the largest number of nonwhite children available for adoption (1235), had 24 nonwhite homes approved for adoption (close to the median of 25 for all agencies combined), whereas in the West South Central region, with the smallest number of nonwhite children (20), 80 nonwhite homes were approved, a figure well above the combined median. Table 2.3 reports the number of white and nonwhite homes for the years between 1967 and 1972.

The figures in Tables 2.2 and 2.3, although from different sources, suggest only general estimated ratios. What is indicated, however, is that by 1972 a historic trend appeared to have been reversed in that the number of ap-

TABLE 2.2   Nonwhite children available and nonwhite approved homes per 100 nonwhite children, by region (185 agencies)

Region	Number	Percentage of All Children	Median Number of Approved Homes
New England	219	11	13
Middle Atlantic	1,235	31	24
East North Central	645	15	25
West North Central	159	12	10
South Atlantic	332	22	42
East South Central	92	25	40
West South Central	20	6	80
Mountain	192	23	50
Pacific	336	19	44
Canada	193	10	19
Total	3,423	19	25

Source: Lucille Grow, A New Look at Supply and Demand in Adoption,

(New York: Child Welfare League of America, 1970), p. 13,

Table 8.

TABLE 2.3 Approved homes per 100 available children, by race and year

| | Number of Approved Homes | | | |
	1967	1970	1971[a]	1972[a]
White	114	116	133	108
Non-white	60	39	39	51

Source:

[a]Opportunity, Division of the Boys and Girls Society of Oregon, August 1973, September 18, 1973, December 2, 1974.

proved white homes decreased sharply from the previous year, falling below the 1967 level, whereas the number of approved nonwhite homes rose. The figures in Table 2.4 represent a considerable improvement over the ones cited in the 1955 study.[7]

As Table 2.4 indicates, after having experienced an approximate 3½-fold increase between 1968 and 1971, the number of transracial adoptions fell sharply thereafter, decreasing 30 percent between 1972 and 1973. Although the number of black inracial adoptions did not experience as dramatic an increase as did transracial adoptions between 1968 and 1971, neither was the 1972–1973 decrease as severe.

Table 2.5 demonstrates the cumulative drop from 1971 through 1974 for both approved adoptive homes and children accepted for adoption. Of interest is that even though over-all white rates declined faster than non-white, this time frame still witnessed voluntary agencies reducing the number of non-white children acceptable for adoption by 35 percent.

Table 2.6 indicates the reaffirmation of a historic trend; the greater availability of acceptable white homes per 100 adoptable white children. The latter is all the more important when one realizes that for this period, as revealed in Table 2.6, fewer white homes were accepted as adoptive placements.

The data in Table 2.7 indicate the ebb and flow of transracial adoption in states that have compiled and released such figures. When examining these

TABLE 2.4 Number of black children placed in white and black homes, 1968–1973

Placement	1968	1969	1970	1971	1972	1973	1972-73(%) Decrease
Total Black Children Placed	3,122	4,336	6,474	7,420	6,065	4,665	23
With black families	2,389	2,889	4,190	4,846	4,467	3,574	20
With white families	733	1,447	2,274	2,574	1,569	1,091	30
Number of Reporting Agencies	194	342	427	468	461	434	

Source: "Some Factors in the Development of Interracial Adoption,"

Opportunity (August, 1973); Opportunity (September 18, 1973);

Opportunity (December 2, 1974).

figures, note that the number in parentheses represents the reporting adoption agencies and that wide discrepancies can be seen (e.g., 72 agencies in Pennsylvania and 2 each in Georgia and New Hampshire).

Many have argued that the ratio between adoptable black children and available black homes is deflated as.a result of a conscious (i.e., racist) effort by white-controlled adoption agencies not to involve the black community more fully in attempting to reach black potential adoptive parents. According to a 1972 study, there is a relationship between the number of adoptable black children on an agency's caseload and the frequency of transracial adoption.[8] An agency that has many available black children is less likely to look for white adoptive parents than an agency that has only a few black children.

The implication is that adoption agencies located in black communities with large constituencies of adoptable black children have more contacts and programs within the black community and are therefore in a better position to locate black adoptive couples.

In a 1972 doctoral dissertation, Dawn Day Wachtel[9] examined the rela-

TABLE 2.5 Decrease in percentage of homes approved for adoption/adoptable children, 1971–1974 (49 voluntary agencies)

Race	Approved Homes	Adoptable Children
White	58	48
Non-white	43	35

*No comparable public agency data available.

Source: Special Report from Child Welfare League of America Research Center, Adoption Trends, 1971-1974, Barbara Haring. (Child Welfare, Vol. LIV, No. 7, July, 1975), pp. 524-25.

tionship between adoption agencies' practices and the placement of black children. Her findings supported the earlier results of David Fanshel[10] and Trudy Bradley[11] indicating that the use of mass media to attract potential adoptive black couples is not an altogether effective method of recruitment. In examining the dropout rate of black couples attracted to adoption agencies by the media (ethnic and nonethnic radio, television, newspapers, etc.) she noted that there was a lower rate of application completion among these individuals than among black applicants who were informally referred. The latter are defined as successful black adoptors who have positive experiences with (black) friends who are themselves potential adoptive parents. Wachtel therefore concluded that the informal system (i.e., word-of-mouth

TABLE 2.6 Approved homes per 100 adoptable children/race, 1971–1974 (49 voluntary agencies)

	White	Non-White
1971	141	79
1974	113	70

*No comparable public agency data available

Source: Special Report from Child Welfare League of America, Research Center, "Adoption Trends, 1971-1974," Barbara Haring. (Child Welfare, Vol. LIV, No. 7, July, 1975), pp. 524-25.

TABLE 2.7 Number of nonwhite children adopted by white families (numbers in parentheses represent reporting adoption agencies)

States	1968	1969	1970	1972	1974
California	70(5)	308(6)	187(19)	215(26)	62(28)
Illinois	42(7)	75(25)	174(33)	56(16)	11(12)
Massachusetts	65(10)	97(16)	149(18)	38(17)	20(13)
Michigan	35(13)	61(16)	161(18)	130(22)	37(27)
Minnesota	76(6)	170(9)	246(9)	64(8)	18(4)
New Jersey	2(4)	29(8)	131(8)	74(9)	38(8)
New York	75(16)	100(31)	168(39)	124(38)	76(52)
Ohio	15(14)	36(33)	95(33)	116(61)	84(51)
Oregon	56(5)	65(7)	81(7)	71(7)	13(4)
Pennsylvania	25(11)	51(36)	137(57)	105(72)	70(60)
Washington	81(6)	106(7)	107(8)	43(5)	9(8)
Wisconsin	45(8)	87(8)	107(8)	61(8)	29(8)
Colorado				32(6)	20(6)
District of Columbia				27(6)	6(4)
Florida				20(7)	27(7)
Indiana				36(9)	28(9)
Iowa				33(10)	17(8)
Maryland				16(19)	11(12)
Tennessee				3(7)	5(10)
Georgia				4(2)	5(2)
New Hampshire				9(2)	6(3)
Total	587	1,185	1,743	1,277	592

Source: Survey by Opportunity: Division of Boys and Girls Aid Society of Oregon. The 1968,1969 and 1970 surveys are reported in National Adoptalk, vol. 5 (November-December, 1969), p. 7; vol. 6 (July-August, 1970), p. 9; vol. 7 (July-August, 1971), p. 9; 1972 in September 18, 1973; 1974 in December 22, 1975.

communication) was the best method by which to ensure eventual black inracial adoption. The difficulty lay in the ability of white-administered adoption agencies to attract enough black adoptors into "the system" in order to establish credibility.

Wachtel's findings have implications when one realizes that, of the 22,000 nonwhite children adopted in 1971, 15,100 were black, and not included in the 15,100 figure were countless thousands (possibly close to 100,000) of other *potentially* adoptable black children who were either in foster care or institutionalized.[12] (Although the Department of Health, Education, and Welfare has issued additional figures for 1972, 1973, and 1974, the number of nonreporting states and states that supplied incomplete data was so large as to make the totals unrepresentative. Therefore 1971 was chosen because of the relative completeness of the data.) It is important to note that there are no national statistics reflecting the number of children *available* for adoption. Data exist only on the number of children *actually* adopted. Wachtel, however, estimated that, in 1971, 3000 black children were legally free for adoption but were not placed with adoptive parents.[13]

Adoption agencies that serve black children predominantly tend to have a higher proportion of black social workers on their staffs than agencies with small populations of black children. Two recent studies revealed that a social worker's race appeared to be one of the strongest factors affecting attitudes toward transracial adoption, with black social workers disapproving more often than white social workers.[14] One study found a correlation of −.85 between the number of white social workers employed and the frequency of inracial adoptions (black-black).[15]

Not only was there a negative correlation between the presence of white social workers on agency staffs and the number of black children adopted by black families (conversely, the more black social workers, the greater the number of inracial black adoptions), but there also appeared to be a negative association between a white social worker's professional contacts (National Association of Social Work membership, attendance at professional meetings, etc.) and his or her agency's involvement with inracial black adoption.[16] This too lends additional support to the hypothesis that agencies with large black clienteles employing black social workers make fewer transracial placements. Although the implication seems valid that agency contacts in the black community and the number of black social workers are related to transracial adoption, these do not appear to be necessary prerequisites for an informed black community. Herzog and Bernstein hypothesized in 1965 that middle-class blacks were no less interested, informed, and disposed toward adoption than middle-class whites.[17] The data suggest that collectively blacks appear to be suspicious, and many are skeptical of any agency's procedures (including adoption agencies),[18] but one cannot link suspicion and skepticism with program awareness.

Evidence seems to suggest that the plight of adoptable black children does not rank high on the list of black adults' social priorities, even when they seem to be aware of the problem's severity.[19] It is about the issue of black inracial adoption that controversy exists. For example, it is argued that, suspiciousness of agencies notwithstanding, middle-class blacks are less apt to adopt because their newly won economic well-being and personal security are defined as tenuous, a definition legitimately born from generations of marginality.[20] This is challenged by others who suggest that with the use of nontraditional types of adoption such as quasi-adoption, subsidized adoption, and so on (see Chapter 7), blacks would adopt at a higher rate.[21] To support the argument that blacks are indeed capable of adopting black children when unencumbered by a white-dominated bureaucracy (e.g., an adoption agency), successful attempts to locate black adoptive families were noted (e.g., Baltimore's Adopt a Black Child and Detroit's Homes for Black Children).[22]

Indeed, financially able nonwhites appear to adopt at a higher rate than whites in similar financial circumstances. Using 1967 adoption figures, the pool of potential adoptive parents can be defined as married couples between the ages of 25 and 44 earning at least $5000 per year. The ratio of prospective nonwhite adoptors to available nonwhite children was then 15.3 per 1000, whereas the ratio for inracial white adoptions was 9.2 per 1000.[23]

However, institutions are condemned for not being more aggressive in their efforts to locate available black adoptive parents.[24] The assumption is that these unknown families are "out there somewhere" and what is required are programs to find them. In fact, in 1973 the CWLA actively supported agency efforts to use the mass media to attract potential minority adoptors: "Recruitment programs should be carried on continually through the various media (such as radio, television, newspapers and magazines) and should include media that reach minority groups."[25]

If the hypothesis is accepted that the desire for economic well being and stability supersedes blacks' willingness to be adoptors, the adoption agencies are "off the hook." In other words, the onus lies on the black community for not adopting black children and not on the policies of adoption agencies or on the individual (white) social worker.

How did this come about? Why were black children not being adopted and why were they forced to remain in foster care or institutionalized when homes appeared to be available and known to adoption agencies? Most, if not all, Oriental children, and to a somewhat lesser degree most American Indian children, managed to be adopted. The answers to these questions lie within the history of transracial adoption itself.

Adoption agencies have historically exercised a good deal of control in establishing, maintaining, and enforcing what can be termed a "worthiness scale" against which potential adoptive couples are measured.[26] Thus couples wanting to adopt healthy white infants when the latter were in available supply would usually have to demonstrate that they had been married for a specific length of time and were of a certain age,[27] religious (attended church),[28] middle-class,[29] in good health (mental and physical),[30] and infertile.[31] Commenting on the "measuring process" whereby agencies establish the criteria by which adoptive applicants are either accepted or rejected, Clayton Hagen, director of the Adoption Unit of Lutheran Social Services in Minnesota said:

The evaluative approach often has extremely negative effects on the adoptive parents. Several years after placement, adoptive couples often retained a distressing amount of hostility toward the agency through which they had adopted. The evaluative approach made the couple's position inherently defensive as they labored to prove that they would be suitable parents. Approaching adoptive applicants as a resource of the agency, and effectively stripping them of rights and responsibilities, did little to enhance their feelings of adequacy.[32]

So strict were the adoption agencies, especially private ones, in enforcing these regulations, that one white couple known to one of us was rejected by an adoption agency because there was a gap of a few months between the time they were civilly married and their church marriage. The adoption agency claimed that this constituted moral indiscretion and denied their application.

GROW AND SHAPIRO STUDY OF WHITE PARENTS WHO ADOPTED BLACK CHILDREN

In 1974, Lucille Grow and Deborah Shapiro of the CWLA published the results of their study of 125 families who had transracially adopted black children.[33] The major purpose of their study was to assess how successful these adoptions had been. The authors explained that they were prepared to measure successful adoptions in the following manner:

How best to evaluate transracial adoptions is a question we may not have answered well, but we did it to the best of our ability. The committee that reviewed our application suggested a comparison group of black children adopted by black families. Serious consideration was given to this, but it was ruled out as unnecessary, since no one had questioned the preferability of within-race adoption if feasible. The question is whether children are better off adopted by parents of a different race than they would be if they lived with neither natural nor adoptive parents. To answer that would necessitate following up black children who had been adopted by white parents and children comparable with the adoptees in all respects except that they had not been adopted. Identifying a comparable sample of non-adopted children did not seem possible.

We therefore confined the research to a descriptive study of adoptions of black or part-black children by white parents. We decided to focus on children who were at least 6 years of age so that they would have had some experience in the community, and on children who had been in their adoptive homes at least 3 years, long enough for initial adjustments to be worked out.[34]

Later, in discussing the specific measures of success they relied on, the authors discussed the techniques employed by other social work researchers who had been confronted with similar problems. Grow and Shapiro commented:

This study of black children adopted by white parents shares the common problem of adoption studies—indeed, of most studies of social programs—that of identifying a valid, operational definition of "success." In an ideal society all adopted children, like their biological peers, would have a happy childhood and develop into well-adjusted, well-functioning adults. In a much-less-than-ideal society, it is evident that many, like their biological peers, will not. Since they do not all become "successful" adults, a series of difficult, usually unanswerable, questions is raised. Is the failure necessarily related to the fact of adoption? Is the rate of failure any different from that observed in the rearing of children by their biological parents? Are the problems of rearing adopted children essentially those inherent in the child-rearing process and subject to the same risks or are they greater? In the specific type of adoption under scrutiny here, is a black child more "successful" in a white adoptive home than he would have been in a black foster home or a series of them?[35]

. . . assessment obviously requires considerable information in a variety of areas and from diverse sources. In this respect, adoption studies also share the dilemmas of child-rearing studies. It is usually not until well into adolescence that children can give valid information about themselves. Their parents, usually the persons best informed about their behavior, are also the most emotionally involved and usually the most biased in their favor. Paper-and-pencil personality tests, which require reading and writing ability on the part of the children, are often not standardized or validated. Tests administered by psychologists and psychiatric evaluations make heavy demands on the research budget, produce more resistance in respondents and also have questionable validity. Seemingly neutral sources of information—case records, social workers' reports, and teachers' evaluations—all have inherent biases and limitations.[36]

The outcome measures developed for this study exploited the possibilities created by the use of computers in which a broad array of different types of data could be used to define different forms of outcome.[37]

In the end, Grow and Shapiro decided on the following measures: (a) the child's responses to the California Test of Personality and the Missouri Children's Behavior Check List Test, (b) three scores based on physical and mental symptoms reported by the parents as present or absent in their child, (c) significant adults' evaluation of the child, that is, mother, father, teachers, and parents' assessment of the child's relations with his or her siblings, and (d) the parents' assessment of the child's attitude toward race.

Note that the only measures that directly reflect the child's opinions and responses were those obtained on the California Test of Personality and the Missouri Children's Behavior Check List Test. All the other scores or outcome measures were derived from the parents' or teachers' evaluation of the child.

On the basis of the children's scores on the California Test of Personality (which purports to measure social and personal adjustment), Grow and Shapiro concluded that the children in their study made about as successful an adjustment in their adoptive homes as other nonwhite children had in prior studies. They claimed that 77 percent of their children had adjusted successfully, and that this percentage is similar to that reported in other studies, some of which are described in Table 2.8.

Table 2.9, from Grow and Shapiro, compares the scores of transracially adopted children with those of adopted white children on the California Test of Personality. A score below the 20th percentile was defined as reflecting poor adjustment, and a score above the 50th percentile was defined as indicating good adjustment. As shown in Table 2.9, the scores of transracially adopted children and those of white adopted children match very closely.

Grow and Shapiro questioned the parents about their expectations concerning their adoptive children's adjustments after adolescence and in adulthood, and the children's ties with them. They report that by and large

TABLE 2.8 Comparison of success rate of transracially adopted versus white children

	Percent
Summarized rate for 11 studies of white infant adoption[a]	78
Racially mixed[b]	72
Japanese[c]	89
Older white[d]	73–78
Indian children[e]	88

Sources:

[a] Alfred Kadushin, "A Study of Adoptive Parents of Hard-to-Place Children," Social Casework, XLIII, no. 5 (1962), pp. 227-33.

[b] Marian Mitchell, "Transracial Adoptions: Philosophy and Practice," Child Welfare, vol. 48, no. 10 (December, 1969), pp. 613-19; Ethel Roskies, "An Exploratory Study of the Characteristics of Adoptive Parents of Mixed Race Children in the Montreal Area," Montreal Star, October 19, 1963.

[c] Andrew Billingsley and Jeanne Giovannoni, "Research Perspectives on Interracial Adoption," in Roger Hiller, ed., Race, Research and Reason (New York: National Association of Social Workers, 1969), p. 58.

[d] Grace Galley, "Interracial Adoptions," Canadian Welfare, vol. 39, no. 6 (November-December, 1963), pp. 248-50.

[e] Harriet Fiske, "Interracial Adoption: The Little Revolution," Social Work, vol. 10, no. 3 (July, 1965), pp. 92-97.

the parents were optimistic. One-third of the parents did not anticipate that their adoptive children would experience future difficulties. In fact, 18 percent did not believe that any trouble lay ahead.

When Grow and Shapiro asked the parents in their survey why they chose to adopt a nonwhite child, 54 percent had reasons and motivations that were essentially social (see Table 2.10). Forty-two percent said they wanted

TABLE 2.9 Total adjustment scores on the California test of Personality of transracially adopted children and white inracial adopted children

Percentile Rank on Test	Transracially Adopted Children	White Adopted Children
	(N=111) %	(N=100) %
2nd	-- ┐	1 ┐
5th	1 │	2 │
10th	6 │ 21	5 │ 22
20th	14 ┘	14 ┘
30th	13	14
40th	19	17
50th	11 ┐	9 ┐
60th	13 │	7 │
70th	10 │	11 │
80th	7 │ 47	7 │ 47
90th	4 │	10 │
95th	2 │	2 │
98th	-- ┘	1 ┘
Total	100	100

Source: Lucille J. Grow and Deborah Shapiro, <u>Black Children, White Parents</u>:
<u>A Study of Transracial Adoption</u>. (Child Welfare League of America,
Inc., 1974), p. 37, Table 2-6.

to provide a home for a hard-to-place child, and 10 percent characterized transracial adoption as a "Christian act."

In support of the idea of providing a family for a hard-to-place child, Table 2.11 suggests that this provision was an important benefit to transracial adoptions. Although there is an 11 percent difference, 49 percent of the mothers and 60 percent of the fathers felt that a benefit of transracial

TABLE 2.10   Reasons for adopting transracially

Reason	Number of Responses	Percent
Social motivation	68	54
Provide a home for hard-to-place child	53	42
Aid to integration; Christian duty	13	10
Integration a benefit to family	2	2
Personal motivation	40	32
Wanted a child, race unimportant	28	22
Became attached to foster child	10	8
Knew child; made parents feel special	2	2
Second choice	14	12
No other children available	12	10
Assurance that child looks Caucasion	2	2
Unclear	3	2
Totals	125	100

Source: Lucille J. Grow and Deborah Shapiro, Black Children, White Parents: A Study of Transracial Adoption. Child Welfare League of America, Inc., 1974, p. 70, Table 3-2.

adoption was that they were able to "give a home to a child whom nobody seemed to want." Seventy-one percent of the mothers and 66 percent of the fathers felt that transracial adoption enabled them "to express the deep love for children . . . [they] . . . have always had." Reinforcing the latter statement, and weighted against the idea of transracial adoption as a gesture to right society's wrongs, was the evidence supplied by the parents that "helping to compensate for the inequities in our society" was not perceived to be very much of a benefit of transracial adoption.

TABLE 2.11 Effects of adoption experience on parents

Possible Benefit	Very Much or Much		A Little		Not at All	
	Mother	Father	Mother	Father	Mother	Father
			(In Percent)			
Has enabled me to give a home to a child whom nobody seemed to want	49	60	26	20	25	20
Has enabled me to fulfill my duty to have a family	16	19	10	15	74	66
Has made me feel less lonely	24	20	19	19	57	61
Has made me feel that I'm doing something toward furthering the cause of an integrated society	31	38	44	41	25	21
Has enabled me to express the deep love for children I have always had	71	66	22	19	7	15
Has brought my spouse and me closer together	19	36	37	32	44	32
Has made me feel more like a "whole" person	34	38	28	30	38	32
Has prevented me from becoming too selfish, too self-centered	27	27	38	41	35	32
Has made me feel that I am helping to compensate for the inequities in our society	23	22	37	46	40	32
Has made my marriage richer	44	54	33	30	23	16
Has made me feel proud about being able to make a contribution to the community	22	24	35	36	43	40
Has given me a great deal of satisfying companionship	79	75	13	15	8	10

Source: Lucille J. Grow and Deborah Shapiro, <u>Black Children, White Parents</u>: <u>A Study of Transracial Adoption</u>. Child Welfare League of America. Inc.. 1974, p. 83, Table 3-5.

Eighty-three percent of the mothers and 82 percent of the fathers said they were not concerned about how their neighbors would react to their adopting a nonwhite child. But, as the data in Table 2.12 suggest, about half of the parents were concerned about how their extended families would react to a transracial adoption.

Grow and Shapiro wanted to find out more about how these parents felt about the concept of transracial adoption. They described four types of transracial adoption and asked which type the parent would encourage or discourage. An "unsure" category was also allowed. As can be seen from Table 2.13, 91 percent of the mothers and a lesser percentage of fathers would encourage transracial adoption by white and black parents or either

TABLE 2.12 Reservations about adopting transracially

Area of Concern	Degree of Concern: Considerable		Moderate		None	
	Mother	Father	Mother	Father	Mother	Father
	(In Percent)					
How it feels to be a parent to an adopted child	2	2	12	14	86	84
How it feels to be a parent to a child of a different race	1	3	10	13	89	84
What extended family's reaction to adoption would be	6	6	17	18	77	76
What extended family's reaction to transracial adoption would be	10	10	35	37	55	53
How black child would fit into family	-	-	23	23	77	77
What neighbors might think	1	1	16	17	83	82
How neighborhood children would treat black child	3	3	36	37	61	60
Whether black child would be happy with white parents	7	7	33	33	60	60

Source: Lucille J. Grow and Deborah Shapiro, Black Children, White Parents: A Study of Transracial Adoption. Child Welfare League of America, Inc., 1974, p. 72, Table 3-3.

TABLE 2.13 Parental convictions about transracial adoptions

Racial Characteristics	Mothers			Fathers		
	En-courage	Unsure	Dis-courage	En-courage	Unsure	Dis-courage
	(In Percent)					
Whites adopting all-black children	65	25	10	67	23	10
Blacks adopting all-white children	59	27	14	61	27	12
Whites adopting part-black children	91	8	1	87	12	1
Blacks adopting part-white children	91	8	1	83	14	3

Source: Lucille J. Grow and Deborah Shapiro, Black Children, White Parents:
A Study of Transracial Adoption. Child Welfare League of America,
Inc., 1974, p. 87, Table 3-7.

part black or part white children, respectively. More uncertainty existed with regard to the other two types of adoption.

Fifty-five percent of the parents who felt some anxiety or had some reservation about the adoption also believed that their adopted child felt some discomfort about being adopted, in contrast to 20 percent of the parents who felt no anxiety about their decision to adopt.

Table 2.14 shows the relationship between the parents' perception of their child's racial discomfort and the child's racial appearance. The more a child appeared to be black, the more the parents felt the child was racially uncomfortable.

In discussing the characteristics of the families in our study, in Chapter 4 we return to a review of Grow and Shapiro's findings and compare the demographic characteristics of the two sets of parents, as well as the attitudes and feelings that motivated them to adopt transracially.

TABLE 2.14   Discomfort about appearance and child's appearance*⁻

Discomfort	Fair, No Negroid features	Fair, Negroid features/ light brown no Negroid features	Light brown or dark, Negroid features
	(In Percent)		
Yes	10	27	42
No	90	73	58
	—	—	—
Total	100	100	100

*Chi-square = 8.01, 2 df, p < .02

Source: Lucille J. Grow and Deborah Shapiro, Black Children, White Parents: A Study of Transracial Adoption.   Child Welfare League of America, Inc., 1974, p. 183, Table 9-1.

THE ANTITRANSRACIAL ADOPTION MOVEMENT

The movement toward accepting transracial adoption as an alternative to leaving certain black children parentless, and the institutionalization of the black struggle for identity and independence crested simultaneously. Each was anathema to the other, and therefore one had to go. Black power aided by white guilt made the weakening of transracial adoption logical. In addition, the transracial adoption of black children (as distinguished from other nonwhite children) was seen by some whites as the least desirable type of adoption. Children who more closely resembled Caucasians were seen as most desirable.[38] Even when the virtues of transracial adoption were extolled (e.g., a family environment is best for any child) and data were presented which indicated that transracially adopted children fared as well as inracially adopted children, it was always noted that the adoption of choice for black children should be in black adoptive homes, with the prognosis that transracially adopted black children may be societally miscast to live in a white world.[39] Provocative articles and statements continued to appear in professional journals questioning the real motivation of whites who adopted transracially. These articles conjured up the specter of cultural genocide, and also suggested that transracially adopted black children would mature into a twilight zone neither white nor black.[40]

At its 1972 national conference, the National Association of Black Social Workers (NABSW) presented a position paper in which transracial adoption was attacked and repudiated. The full text is included in an appendix to this chapter, but the following excerpt establishes the flavor of the attack.

Black children should be placed only with black families whether in foster care or adoption. Black children belong physically, psychologically and culturally in Black families in order that they receive the total sense of themselves and develop a sound projection of their future. . . . Black children in white homes are cut off from the healthy development of themselves as Black people.

The socialization process for every child begins at birth. Included in the socialization process is the child's cultural heritage which is an important segment of the total process. This must begin at the earliest moment; otherwise our children will not have the background and knowledge which is necessary to survive in a racist society. This is impossible if the child is placed with white parents in a white environment. . . .

We [the members of the NABSW] have committed ourselves to go back to our communities and work to end this particular form of genocide [transracial adoption].

The popular black press, especially *Ebony,* continued to feature articles in which adoption and transracial adoption were the central themes.[41] These were wide-ranging reports attempting to present the gamut of positions and ramifications involved in black adoption. Their purpose one would suspect was to keep this question alive in the minds of their constituents and lay bare the arguments surrounding the transracial adoption of black children by white families. In August 1974, an entire special issue of *Ebony* was devoted to the black child with the adoption controversy woven throughout several reports.[42]

The following response is representative of the tone of many of the readers' letters that were published in *Ebony* following that issue:

This is a white racist society caused by whites and whites alone, and their act of adopting blacks is insulting and psychologically damaging and dangerous. For four hundred years, we have been constantly bombarded with overt and institutionalized racism, which white people to this present day have done little to correct. I wonder how Jews would feel if ex-Nazis rushed to adopt little Jewish orphans.

It's ironic; once whites enslaved us because they considered themselves superior, and still do, now they want to "rear and love us." Why?[43]

Transracial adoption was defined originally not as a program to salvage black children from the effects of foster placement or institutionalization, but as a way of fulfilling the needs of childless white couples, given the dwindling availability of white children.[44] Thus it was seen as a white enterprise instituted for the advantage of the white community.[45] In addition, it was referred to as demeaning and a blatant attempt by whites to further render black people impotent.

The latter part of the 1960s witnessed a major attack on transracial adoption organized by leaders of black organizations and by black social workers. By mid-1971 the pronouncements against the practice of transracial adoption, by both black and nonblack organizations, became more political and provocative. NABSW stated in unequivocal terms that black children belong in black homes and only the latter can properly prepare a child to deal with his or her blackness.[46] An American Indian organization essentially echoed the statement of NABSW, substituting "American Indian" for "black."[47] In 1974 the Black Caucus of the North American Conference on Adoptable Children recommended "support [for] the consciousness development movement of all groups" and "that every possible attempt should be made to place black and other minority children in a cultural and racial setting similar to their original group." In May 1975, the dean of the Howard University School of Social Work, president of the NABSW, stated that "black children who grow up in white homes end up with white psyches."[48]

Some felt that black adoptive homes did exist, if only adoption agencies would make more strenuous efforts to locate them, changing what essentially are racist criteria, and that efforts should be made to prevent black children from entering white homes.[49]

A few groups, especially the Open Door Society, along with individual families who had transracially adopted, mounted a somewhat muted campaign to refute the forebodings of those in opposition to transracial adoption,[50] although clearly the media gave the anti forces more attention.

Some professional black organizations took no stance at all on transracial adoption. In a survey conducted for this monograph, a limited number of such organizations was asked to furnish statements regarding transracial adoption. Of the responding groups, the National Medical Association,

Black Caucus, United Federation of Teachers, and Committee of Black Psychiatrists, none indicated that any had been made.

In one of the more moderate attacks on transracial adoption, Leon Chestang in the May 1972 issue of *Social Work* posed a series of critical questions for white parents who had adopted or who were considering adopting a black child:

The central focus of concern in biracial adoption should be the prospective adoptive parents. Are they aware of what they are getting into? Do they view their act as purely humanitarian, divorced from its social consequences? Such a response leaves the adoptive parents open to an overwhelming shock when friends and family reject and condemn them. Are they interested in building world brotherhood without recognizing the personal consequences for the child placed in such circumstances? Such people are likely to be well meaning but unable to relate to the child's individual needs. Are the applicants attempting to solve a personal or social problem through biracial adoption? Such individuals are likely to place an undue burden on the child in resolving their problems.

And what of the implications for the adoptive family of living with a child of another race? The negative societal traits attributed to blacks are likely to be inherited by the adoptive family, thereby subjecting the family to insults, racial slurs, and ostracism.

The white family that adopts a black child is no longer a "white family." In the eyes of the community its members become traitors, nigger-lovers, do-gooders, rebels, oddballs, and, most significantly, ruiners of the community. Unusual psychological armaments are required to shield oneself from the behavioral and emotional onslaught of these epithets.[51]

But Chestang concluded his piece on a more optimistic note than most critics of transracial adoption. "Who knows what problems will confront the black child reared by a white family and what the outcome will be?" he asked. "But these children, if they survive, have the potential for becoming catalysts for society in general."

Somewhere between the pro and anti forces stood the CWLA, an organization in which most adoption agencies hold membership. Member agencies, however, are not bound to the league's principles, but the latter do reflect the "best" in standard setting. Since 1958 their SAS has included a statement on the racial background of the adoptee and the adoptors. The development of their position on the racial issue by and large reflects the change in thinking within the field. In 1958, although stating that race alone should not be the most persuasive argument determining a child's adoptive parents, the SAS indicated that "children placed in adoptive families with similar racial characteristics . . . can become more easily integrated.[52] With reference to physical makeup, the SAS suggested that it should not be a criterion upon which an adoptive family is chosen, "with the possible exception of . . . color."[53]

In 1968, with regard to race, the SAS indicated again that race should not be the sole determinant in choosing adoptive parents, but this time with the proviso that it would be erroneous to assume that conflict would inevitably follow should a child be transracially adopted. In fact, the SAS appeared to go one step further and indicated that adoption agencies "should be ready to help families who wish to adopt children of another race" and, given families who appear willing and able to adopt transracially, "such couples should be encouraged to consider such a child."[54] When speaking of physical makeup, the SAS assumed a much broader approach. Instead of indicating that color was a "possible exception" in the selection of potential adoptive parents, the 1968 statement indicated simply that "physical resemblances . . . should not be a determining factor in the selection of a home."[55]

By 1973, the circle was complete. While accepting transracial adoption as one type of placement, the SAS stated that, given the tenor of the times, always an apparent powerful influence on the league's standards, it was preferable to place children in families of their own racial background: "In today's social climate children placed in adoptive families with similar racial characteristics can become more easily integrated. . . ."[56] Thus the CWLA appears to have accepted the position that, all things being equal, black children, for everyone's sake, would be better served in black homes.

In 1975 Comer and Poussaint posited that, although all children have to develop a sense of self-worth, black children especially need this to offset the effects of racism. They also felt that black parents must educate their children to recognize and cope with a different set of issues with which white parents and their children do not have to deal.[57] These statements seem to bolster the position that the transracial adoption of black children by white parents will in all probability lead to their being ill-suited to handle certain life experiences adequately.

Perhaps the question of the "rightness" or "wrongness" of transracial adoption, either in the short or long run, can best be understood by investigating the statements made by various organizations representing different interests. In other words, by whose standards—those of transracially adopting parents, nonwhite individuals and organizations, or the black children—and by what measures—the transracially adopted child's ultimate racial identity, his or her personal adjustment in later life, or as an immediate solution for the condition of parentless children—will transracial adoption be judged? Recall the story of the three blind men and the elephant. Each man probed a different portion of the elephant, and each described a different object.

The position of the individuals and groups who oppose transracial adoption has been presented in previous discussions. One can argue from their perspective that not only is transracial adoption a modern-day version of cultural genocide and an act of agency duplicity and continuing white paternalism, but an extension of the class struggle starting from slavery.[58]

However, the statements of the organizations and individuals (especially the adopting parents) supporting transracial adoption can best be reviewed by recalling the rationale that such adoptions are humanitarian acts, defined purely and simply by love and compassion for another human being. To a somewhat lesser degree it was seen as a blow against racism and, as with any other type of adoption, a gesture against overpopulation. Transracial adoption was never defined by any individual or organization advocating its ideology as an attempt to diminish, in any manner, a nonwhite child's identification with his or her own race.

But the arguments raised by those in opposition to transracial adoption stem in large measure from prior experience with a hostile white world and suspicion borne of generations of subjugation. On the face of it, from the opponents' perspective, the raising of black children in white homes smacks of the paternalism that has defined white-black relations for so long.

Among inracially adopted children, as compared with nonadopted children, if emotional disturbance, one of the most popular indicators of success, is used, the data are at times contradictory. Some feel that there is no real difference in the amount of emotional disturbance in inracially adopted children as compared with nonadopted children.[59] Others contend that adopted children are more likely than nonadopted children to be emotionally disturbed or suffer from personality disorders.[60] Therefore, within the overall field of inracial adoption, there seem to be inconsistencies regarding the adjustment of adopted children at the time they were tested.

With regard to the eventual adult racial identity and personal adjustment of these children, the jury is still out. At the present time data on enough adults who have been transracially adopted are just not available to permit any final conclusions. One can only speculate on the basis of limited evidence as to what the end results will be. Even though many unknowns continue to exist militating against accurate prediction as to these childrens'

final racial identity, present data, although suggestive, indicate that transracially adopted children will not be lost to their respective races. On the
contrary, some data suggest that these children are quite aware of and
sensitive to their racial identity. Further discussion of these issues appears in
Section Two.

APPENDIX: POSITION PAPER DEVELOPED FROM WORKSHOPS CONCERNING TRANSRACIAL ADOPTION*

The Workshop on Trans-Racial Adoption that met during the National
Association of Black Social Workers' Conference has taken a position
against the practice of trans-racial adoption of Black children.

During this three day workshop, we have taken the position that Black
children should be placed only with Black families whether in foster care or
for adoption. Black children belong, physically, psychologically and culturally in Black families in order that they receive the total sense of themselves
and develop a sound projection of their future. Human beings are products
of their environment and develop their sense of values, attitudes and self
concept within their family structures. Black children in white homes are cut
off from the healthy development of themselves as Black people.

Our position is based on:

1. the necessity of self-determination from birth to death, of all Black
   people.
2. the need of our young ones to begin at birth to identify with all Black
   people in a Black community.
3. the philosophy that we need our own to build a strong nation.

The socialization process for every child begins at birth. Included in the
socialization process is the child's cultural heritage which is an important
segment of the total process. This must begin at the earliest moment;
otherwise our children will not have the background and knowledge which
is necessary to survive in a racist society. This is impossible if the child is
placed with white parents in a white environment.

White institutions have repeatedly stated that they are using new methods

---

* From the position paper developed at the National Association of Black Social Workers'
Conference in Nashville, Tenn., April 4–9, 1972.

to find "good" Black homes; white institutions lack the ability to determine a "good" Black home. This violates our rights as a group of people to determine our own destiny and ignores the Black family as an institution with legitimate values of its own.

The aforementioned fact is proved false again when social workers testified that when a small amount of effort is put forth, we can find strong, healthy and loving Black families. Black workers in private and government agencies stated that their programs have been very successful when they have sought Black adoptive parents.

As we deliberated on the strengths of the Black family, we reinforced the validity of the single parent family, the grandparent family and other instances of the extended family, thereby re-affirming the existence of all that is needed for the placement of our children within the Black community.

Black social workers must be in the vanguard of Black community activity toward ending the practice of trans-racial placements of Black children. We enumerated various strategies toward self-education and public education relative to the problem and directions for specific program planning. They are listed as follows:

1. Confrontations with agencies in our communities based upon the solid facts presented at this conference.
2. Education of all workers to our rights to determine where our children are placed. We might add that education means continuously and not one hour during an inservice-training session.
3. Education of all workers about the uniqueness of Black families.
4. Development of educational programs that will stimulate increased adoptive activity within the Black community.
5. Work closely with the staff, administration and boards of directors of our agencies to change the policies and procedures that support trans-racial placements of our children.
6. To work closely with community groups and adoptive parents.
7. To monitor such groups as ARENA and Open Door Society.
8. Development of special recruitment programs within and outside of our agencies to locate Black homes.
9. Develop a communication network that will facilitate an exchange of information among participants of this workshop. The Afro-American Family and Community Services (440 West Division, Chicago, Illinois 60610) has agreed to undertake this responsibility.

10. We will attend and caucus at the Third North American Conference on Adoptable Children April 21–23, St. Louis, Missouri. There we will make known our position. Tentatively, the Greater St. Louis Chapter has agreed to coordinate an agenda for this activity.

11. To be knowledgeable of national and local laws concerning foster care and adoptions.

12. We must be about the business of protecting the Black family and Black community as a legitimate and viable institution.

We the participants of the workshop have committed ourselves to go back to our communities and work to end this particular form of genocide. We have agreed to use the alternatives to trans-racial adoption presented at our conference and to develop other alternatives and ways of implementation if necessary based upon our experience as Black people.

NOTES

1. In 1961 there were approximately 32,127 blacks living in all of Canada (0.02 percent of the population). *Canadian Yearbook*, Canadian Government, 1966, p. 201, Table 14.
2. Elizabeth Shepherd, "Adopting Negro Children: White Families Find It Can Be Done," *New Republic* (June 20, 1964), pp. 10–12; Harriet Fricke, "Interracial Adoption: The Little Revolution," *Social Work*, vol. 10, no. 3 (July 1965), pp. 92–97.
3. Bernice Madison and Michael Shapiro, "Black Adoption—Issues and Policies," *The Social Service Review*, vol. 47, no. 4 (December 1973), pp. 531–554.
4. "The Parents Who Wait," *Chicago Daily News*, August 23, 1975, p. 25.
5. Michael Shapiro, *A Study of Adoption Practices*, vol. 3: *Adoption of Children with Special Needs*, Child Welfare League of America, New York, 1957.
6. Lucille J. Grow, *A New Look at Supply and Demand in Adoption*, Child Welfare League of America, New York, 1970, p. 9.
7. Shapiro, *op. cit.*, footnote 5.
8. Andrew Billingsley and Jeanne M. Giovannoni, *Children of the Storm: Black Children and American Child Welfare*, Harcourt, New York, 1972, p. 198.
9. Dawn Day Wachtel, "Adoption Agencies and the Adoption of Black Children: Social Change and Equal Opportunity in Adoption," dissertation, University of Michigan, Ann Arbor, 1972, p. 84.
10. David Fanshel, *A Study in Negro Adoption*, Child Welfare League of America, New York, 1957.
11. Trudy Bradley, "An Exploration of Caseworkers' Perception of Adoptive Applicants," *Child Welfare*, vol. 45 (October 1966), pp. 433–43.
12. Department of Health, Education, and Welfare, *Program Statistics and Data Systems*, NCSS Report E-10 SRS, May 23, 1973.
13. Wachtel, *op. cit.*, footnote 9, p. 24.
14. Anne Stern Ferber, "Attitudes of Adoption Workers toward Requests for Transracial Adop-

tions," research project, University of Maryland, School of Social Work and Community Planning, Baltimore, 1972; Dawn Day Wachtel, "White Social Workers and the Adoption of Black Children," paper presented at the August 1973 meetings of the American Sociological Association, New York.

15. Wachtel, *op. cit.*, footnote 14.

16. *Ibid.*

17. Elizabeth Herzog and Rose Bernstein, "Why So Few Negro Adoptions?" *Children*, vol. XLL (1965), pp. 14–18.

18. Leila Calhoun Deasy and Olive Westbrooke Quinn, "The Urban Negro and Adoption of Children," *Child Welfare*, vol. XLI (November 1962), pp. 400–407; Martha Perry, "An Experiment in Recruitment of Negro Adoptive Parents," *Social Casework*, vol. 39 (May 1958), pp. 292–97; Mary Louise Sharrar, "Attitude of Black Natural Parents Regarding Adoption," *Child Welfare*, vol. L (May 1971), pp. 286–89.

19. Elizabeth Herzog, Cecelia Sudia, Jan Harwood, and Carol Newcomb, *Families for Black Children: The Search for Adoptive Parents—An Experience Survey*, Cooperative Report of the Division of Research and Evaluation, Children's Bureau, Office of Child Development, and Social Research Group, George Washington University, Washington, D.C., 1971.

20. Deasy and Quinn, *op. cit.*, footnote 18; Irving A. Fowler, "The Urban Middle Class Negro and Adoption: Two Series of Studies and Their Implications for Action," *Child Welfare*, vol. 45, no. 9 (March 1972), pp. 522–525.

21. Robert Andrews, "Permanent Placement of Negro Children through Quasi-Adoption," *Child Welfare*, vol. 47 (December 1968), pp. 583–586, 613.

22. Clarence D. Fischer, "Homes for Black Children," *Child Welfare*, vol. L, no. 2 (February 1971), pp. 108–111; Ruth H. Young, "Adoption of Black Children: An Assessment of the ABCD Project in Maryland," University of Maryland, School of Social Work and Community Planning, Baltimore, 1971.

23. *Adoptions in 1967, Supplement to Child Welfare Statistics—1967*, Children's Bureau Statistical Series 92 (Washington, DC, US Department of Health, Education and Welfare, 1968); *Current Population Reports*, Series, P-60, #59 (April, 1969), Bureau of Census.

24. Edmond Jones, "On Transracial Adoption of Black Children," *Child Welfare*, vol. LI, no. 3 (March 1972), pp. 156–164, 158.

25. Child Welfare League of America, *Standards of Adoption Service*, revised, Child Welfare League of America, New York, 1973, p. 93, Section 6.11.

26. Henry Maas, "The Successful Adoptive Parent Applicant," *Social Work*, vol. 5, no. 1 (January 1960), pp. 14–20; Helen Fradkin, "Adoptive Parents for Children With Special Needs," *Child Welfare*, vol. 37, no. 1 (January 1958), pp. 1–6.

27. Michael Shapiro, *A Study of Adoption Practice*, vol. 1: *Adoption Agencies and the Children They Serve*, Child Welfare League of America, New York, 1956, pp. 75, 80–83.

28. Child Welfare League of America, *Standards for Adoption Service*, Child Welfare League of America, New York, 1958, p. 25, Section 4.9, *ibid.*, footnote, pp. 76–86.

29. Florence G. Brown, "What Do We Seek in Adoptive Parents," *Social Casework*, vol. 32, no. 4 (1951), pp. 155–161.

30. Child Welfare League of America, *op. cit.*, footnote 27, pp. 75, 87.

31. *Ibid.*, pp. 75–76.

32. David C. Anderson, *Children of Special Value: Interracial Adoption in America*, St. Martin's, New York, 1971, p. 169.

33. Lucille J. Grow and Deborah Shapiro, *Black Children, White Parents: A Study of Transracial Adoption*, Child Welfare League of America, New York, 1974.

34. *Ibid.*, p. ii.

35. *Ibid.*, p. 89.

36. *Ibid.*, p. 90.

37. *Ibid.*, p. 94.
38. Donald E. Chambers, "Willingness to Adopt Atypical Children," *Child Welfare*, vol. 49, no. 5 (May 1970), pp. 275–279.
39. Ursula M. Gallagher, "Adoption Resources for Black Children," *Children*, vol. 18, no. 2 (March–April 1971), pp. 49–53.
40. Leon Chestang, "The Dilemma of Bi-Racial Adoption," *Social Work*, vol. XVII (May, 1972), pp. 100–105; Edmund D. Jones, "On Transracial Adoption of Black Children," *Child Welfare*, vol. 51 (March 1972), pp. 156–164; Joseph Morganstern, "The New Face of Adoption," *Newsweek* (September 13, 1971), pp. 66–72.
41. Helen H. King, "It's Easier to Adopt Today," *Ebony* (December 1970), p. 120.
42. *Ebony*, special issue on the black child (August 1974).
43. *Ebony*, letter to the editor (August 1974).
44. Billingsley and Giovannoni, *op. cit.*, footnote 8.
45. Andrew Billingsley, review of E. R. Braithwaite's *Paid Servant*, McGraw-Hill, New York, 1969, in *Social Work*, vol. 13, no. 4 (October 1968), pp. 106–109.
46. *New York Times*, April 23, 1971, p. 75; April 9, 1972, p. 29; April 10, 1972, p. 27; April 12, 1972, p. 38; April 23, 1972, p. 111.
47. *Ann Arbor News*, July 17, 1972, p. 10.
48. Sandy Banisky, "The Question: Is It Bad for Black Children to Be Adopted by Whites," *Baltimore Sun*, May 28, 1975, p. B1.
49. *Ibid.*
50. M. Edgar, "Black Children, White Parents: A Problem of Identity," unpublished paper of the Open Door Society, Montreal, Canada, 1973.
51. Chestang, *op. cit.*, footnote 40.
52. Child Welfare League of America, *Standards for Adoption Service*, Child Welfare League of America, New York, 1958, pp. 24, Section 4.6.
53. *Ibid.*, p. 26, Section 4.11.
54. Child Welfare League of America, *Standards for Adoption Service*, revised, Child Welfare League of America, 1973, p. 34, Section 4.5.
55. Child Welfare League of America, *Standards for Adoption Service*, revised, Child Welfare League of America, New York, 1968, p. 35, Section 4.9.
56. *Ibid.*, p. 92, Section 4.5.
57. James P. Comer and Alvin F. Poussaint, *Black Child Care*, Simon and Schuster, New York, 1975.
58. Eugene D. Genovese, *Roll, Jordan, Roll: The World the Slaves Made*, Pantheon, New York, 1974.
59. Barbara Raleigh, "Adoption As a Factor in Child Guidance," *Smith College Studies in Social Work*, vol. 25, no. 1 (October 1974), p. 53; Dolores M. Sweeney, Diane T. Gasboro, and Martin Gluck, "A Descriptive Study of Adopted Children Seen in a Child Guidance Center," *Child Welfare*, vol. 42, no. 9 (November 1963), pp. 345–349; Elizabeth A. Lawder, Janet Hoopes, Robert G. Andrews, Katherine D. Lower, and Susan Y. Perry, *A Follow-up Study of Adoptions Post Placement Functioning of Adoption Families*, Child Welfare League of America, New York, 1970.
60. For an excellent discussion, see Alfred Kadushin, "Adoptive Parenthood: A Hazardous Adventure?," *Social Work*, vol. 11, no. 3 (July 1966), pp. 30–39; see also Povl W. Toussieng, "Thoughts Regarding the Etiology of Psychological Difficulties in Adopted Children," *Child Welfare*, vol. 41, no. 2 (February 1962), pp. 59–65, 71; Marshall Shecter, "Observations on Adopted Children," *Archives of General Psychiatry*, vol. 111, no. 1 (July 1960), pp. 21–32; Edgar F. Borgatta and David Fanshel, *Behavioral Characteristics of Children Known to Psychiatric Outpatient Clinics*, Child Welfare League of America, New York, 1965.

CHAPTER THREE

ADOPTION OF AMERICAN INDIAN
AND ASIAN CHILDREN
BY WHITE PARENTS

The two largest groups of children other than American blacks involved in transracial adoption, although their numbers nowhere approach that of black children, are American Indians and Orientals. The recently arrived Vietnamese constitute the largest bloc in the latter category.

Whereas American Indian children were involved in the normal adoptive process, Vietnamese, and to a much lesser degree, Cambodian children, were "imported" into this country in a dramatic fashion under unique and often dubious conditions. By and large, the voluntary transracial adoption of American Indian children, even by adoptive parents living in distant parts of the United States posed no special political difficulties. It was not until the early 1970s, almost a decade and a half after the beginning of the adoption of American Indian children by white parents, that cries of cultural genocide were uttered by tribal leaders. These cries sounded much like the more organized opposition to transracial adoption launched by black social workers.[1]

The transracial adoption of Vietnamese children was perceived as a direct consequence of failure in foreign policy. Once again, as in earlier situations involving the transfer of European, Japanese, and Korean children (see Chapter 1), adoption was viewed as an example of national expiation. Some opponents of transracial adoption attempted to draw the expiation analogy in regard to any type of transracial adoption, including the transracial adoption of American black and Indian children.

This chapter describes the conditions that made American Indian and Vietnamese children available for transracial adoption and reviews the findings of studies that describe the adjustment of these children and their parents to the adoption.

AMERICAN INDIAN CHILDREN

Without chronicling the multitude of injustices the American Indians suffered at the hands of white Americans, these people, after being colonialized and historically humiliated, were then treated as invisible. Their children, too, have not been spared this dubious distinction.[2]

Although unseen, in the sense that they have been removed from their lands and communities and shunted onto federally administered reservations, American Indians have not been immune to the life-style that produces a "disadvantaged" racial minority. Indeed they appear to be its model. By any measure of success—life expectancy, income, education, housing, legitimacy rates, medical and social service availability and so on—the American Indian ranks among the lowest.

The literature describing the adoptive practices, conventional or transracial, of American Indians, supports the "invisible person" doctrine. Until the 1960s there was little mention, statistical, or otherwise,[3] of any major adoption study involving American Indian children. Save for a few who were transracially adopted as part of the hesitant testing of the transracial adoption waters in the United States and Canada,[4] it was not until 1972, when David Fanshel's *Far from the Reservation* was published, that any type of large-scale adoption program and research project serving and describing predominately American Indians appeared in the literature.[5]

The Indian Adoption Project, the program described in Fanshel's work, resulted from a 1957 study which indicated the legal availability of 1000 American Indian children for adoption, who were living either in foster care or in institutions. The project, which lasted from September 1958 to December 1967, was a joint effort sponsored by the Bureau of Indian Affairs and the CWLA (neither of which is an adoption agency) initially to promote nationwide conventional and transracial adoptions of between 50 and 100 American Indian children. At its conclusion in 1968, when most of its activities were subsumed by the Adoption Resource Exchange of North America (ARENA), the project had successfully placed 395 children from 11 states. Ninety-seven of these children were adopted by white families living in 15 different states. *Far from the Reservation* is an examination of the adjustment patterns of these 97 children and their adoptive white parents.

Articles written in the 1960s, especially those by Arnold Lyslo, director of the Indian Adoption Project, describe some of the initial attempts at and success of transracial adoption of American Indian children. These articles examine a series of related adoption programs, many of which were to be incorporated into the Indian Adoption Project. For example, in 1960 Lyslo reported that, of 14 Indian children available for adoption, 13 had been placed with white adoptive parents and 1 with an Indian family. In an attempt to dispel popular beliefs, he cautioned against assuming that tribal mores automatically allowed the ready acceptance of out-of-wedlock children into the (extended) family and urged agencies to make potential adoptive parents aware of the availability of American Indian children.[6]

In 1961, Lyslo stated that 30 Indian children had been adopted, mostly by white couples living in areas geographically distant from the reservations. One can legitimately speculate that community attitudes and racial prejudice on the part of those living closer to the reservations prevented them from adopting Indian children. Most of the 30 children described above were adopted through northeastern agencies. Another reason why so few Indian children were available for adoption to anyone, anywhere, was the opposition, in varying degrees, on the part of some tribes to sanction intertribal adoptions, let alone transracial adoptions.[7] By 1964 a total of 150 Indian children had been adopted transracially, mostly by families who lived in eastern states.

About this time some of the initial results from the second part of the

Indian Adoption Project were being reported. They focused on the adjustment patterns of the 150 children and their adoptive parents.[8] It appeared that the degree of tribal acculturation and the availability of social services were strongly associated with positive feelings toward transracial adoption on the part of tribal representatives. Most of the adoptive parents were described in the reports as being motivated by humanitarian and religious principles and appeared to be making successful adjustments to their children and their community.[9] The children also seemed to be adjusting to their new society.

In 1967, Lyslo reported the results of a mailed questionnaire survey sent by the CWLA to 102 adoption agencies with significant Indian populations.[10] This survey was independent of the Indian Adoption Project. The results from the adoption agencies indicated that the majority of Indian children were being transracially adopted by white families. Of 1128 Indian children available for adoption, 66 of the 90 reporting agencies indicated that 696 had been adopted, 584 of whom had been placed with white families. Only 14 were adopted by Indian couples. Thirty-two children had been adopted by couples with one Indian parent. The remainder had been placed with nonwhite, non-Indian families (e.g., black, Mexican, Spanish-American). Several of the adoption agencies implied that, were it not for state racial prejudice, more Indian children could have been transracially adopted. Four of the state agencies reported that several tribes, the Hopi, Navajo, Pueblo, and Colorado River were reluctant to have their children adopted by non-Indian families.[11]

In 1972, *Far from the Reservation*, by David Fanshel, was published. This work stands as the major research effort undertaken thus far to report the experiences of transracially adopted American Indian children and their parents. In the paragraphs that follow we review some of Fanshel's major findings, because his work represents both the most important and the most recent effort on this topic.

On the whole, Fanshel saw in the results of his study grounds for cautious optimism. In Table 3.1 we see that he divided his families into seven adjustment levels and distributed them according to the degree to which the parents reported that they believed their adopted child had made the adjustment described at each level.

The distribution shows that only 10 percent of the parents perceived their children's future adjustment as "guarded" (Level 5), and only one child was seen to have a "dim" (Level 6) future. In Fanshel's words, "More than fifty percent of the children were rated as showing relatively problem-free ad-

TABLE 3.1 Level of adjustment perceived by white parents of American Indian children

Number	Percent	Description of Level
10	10	Level One (Child is making an excellent adjustment in all spheres--the outlook for his future adjustment is excellent.)
41	43	Level Two
24	25	Level 3 (Child is making an adequate adjustment-- his strengths outweigh the weaknesses he shows--the outlook for his future adjustment is hopeful.)
10	10	Level Four
10	10	Level Five (Child is making a mixed adjustment-- generally the problems he faces are serious and the outlook for his future adjustment is guarded.)
1	1	Level Six
None	None	Level Seven (Child is making an extremely poor adjustment--the outlook for his future adjustment is unpromising.)

Source: David Fanshel, Far from the Reservation: The Transracial Adoption of American Indian Children. (Metuchem, N.J.: Scarecrow Press, 1972), p.280

justments (Levels 1 and 2) and another twenty-five percent were rated as showing adequate adjustment with strengths outweighing weaknesses (Level 3). Another ten percent of the children were rated at Level 4—located midway between adjustments regarded as adequate and those viewed as guarded."[12] Many of the parents acknowledged that difficulties lay ahead, and that they expected that those difficulties would surface when their children reached adolescence and adulthood. Many felt that the difficulties would be proportional to the "full-bloodedness" of their children; and therefore children who appeared less distinctively Indian would have less turbulent experiences. The existence of anxiety or lack of it therefore rested on the degree to which the children were of mixed blood.

In examining which social and demographic factors correlated best with the parents' perceptions of the child's adjustment, Fanshel found the strongest relationship between age and adjustment. The older the child at the time of initial placement, the more difficult the adjustment. Fanshel also discovered an association between age at placement and parental strictness, noting that the older the child the more strict the adoptive parents tended to be.

It is important to emphasize that all these impressions were based on the parents' responses to their children's adjustment over three different time periods. The professional evaluation of parental impressions (referred to as the Overall Child Adjustment Rating) was the yardstick by which the childrens' adjustments were viewed, and it served as the basis for predictions for the future. At no time did Fanshel involve the children in attempting to predict future adjustments.

The child's sex appeared minimally related to adjustment, boys being defined as slightly more problematic than girls. A family's social position was also related to the child's adjustment.[13] The higher the family's status the more difficulty the child seemed to experience, and therefore the more problematic his or her behavior. Fanshel explained this phenomenon by suggesting that parents of higher socioeconomic status set higher standards of behavior for their children, and thus have higher expectations of adoption. There was no relationship between the parents' religious affiliation or degree of religiousness and a child's adjustment.

When the parents were questioned about their willingness to adopt "a child of mixed Negro-white parentage" who was "obviously Negro in features and skin color" and about their willingness to adopt "a child of mixed Negro-white parentage" who was "not obviously Negro in appearance," Fanshel found that 58 percent of the mothers and 46 percent of the fathers would not consider an "obviously Negro" child. Forty-seven percent of the mothers and 30 percent of the fathers also would not consider a child who was "not obviously Negro" in appearance. Table 3.2 describes the distribution of responses for the mothers and fathers.[14] About two-thirds of the parents would not consider or would have major reservations about adopting a "Negro" child, whatever his or her skin shade and appearance.

In his conclusion, Fanshel addressed the issue of whether or not the transracial adoption of American Indian children should be encouraged.[15]

TABLE 3.2 Types of children parents could consider adopting by skin shade

Question	Response Categories	Mothers' Response	Fathers' Response
A child of mixed	Could not consider	57.9	45.5
Negro-white parentage	Major reservations	20.0	27.8
(obviously Negro in	Minor Reservations	6.3	16.7
features and skin	Adopt easily	15.8	10.0
color)		100.0	100.0
Same as above but	Could not consider	47.4	29.7
not obviously	Major reservations	15.8	24.2
Negro in appearance	Minor reservations	14.7	28.6
	Adopt easily	22.1	17.5
		100.0	100.0

Source: Fanshel, Far from the Reservation, pp. 128, 179,
Table V-8 and Table VI-8.

He described the costs involved in transracial adoption and concluded that adoption was cheaper than foster care or institutionalization. He established that the children were secure and loved in their adoptive homes. He found that the adoptive parents were happy and satisfied with their children. Nevertheless, in the end, he concluded that the decision as to whether the practice should or should not continue would be made on political grounds, and not on the basis of the quality of the adjustment that parents and children experienced.

Since the publication of Far from the Reservation in 1972, practically no additional information has appeared in the professional literature regarding the transracial adoption of American Indian children. Some data may be found in the periodic newsletters published by various organizations concerned with both conventional and transracial adoption.[16] These data, however, are usually presented as general categories, and detail is, by and large, lacking. For example, in the 1975 annual report of ARENA, one notes that of 238 white, black, Indian, Oriental, and Spanish children who were adopted, 120 were American Indian. One cannot tell, however, whether any of these Indian children were transracially adopted.

It seems reasonable to assume that the limited momentum achieved by the transracial adoption movement as it relates to American Indian children is on the decline. American Indians, like other racial minorities, probably will continue to organize and demonstrate (as in the 1973 "occupation" of Wounded Knee, South Dakota, by members of the American Indian Movement) in order to reawaken both their own and white America's attention to their historic rights. The resurgence of Indian consciousness will undoubtedly lead toward viewing the transracial adoption of their children as yet another form of humiliation—in the explosive jargon of the 1970s "as a final contemptuous form of robbery."

VIETNAMESE CHILDREN

As a result of the Vietnamese war, an estimated 800,000 to 1,500,000 children were made homeless and/or orphaned. Of this figure, about 25,000 to 100,000 children were fathered by American soldiers. Half of these "mixed" children had black fathers.[17]

Such agencies as the Travelers Aid International, Social Services of America, Catholic Relief Service, Welcome House, Friends of All Children, and the Holt Adoption Program were actively involved in attempting to locate American families willing to adopt Vietnamese children. Their efforts, however, were thwarted by the severe restrictions placed on them by the South Vietnamese government, restrictions not too unlike the traditionally rigid eligibility policies of American adoption agencies (i.e., requirements based on age, income, marital status, number of children already in the home).

During the period 1964–1973, approximately 1130 Vietnamese children were adopted by American families.[18] In 1974, the combined efforts of the Holt Adoption Program and Travelers Aid International accounted for an increase of between 500 to 600 Vietnamese children.[19] From 1972 to 1974 the Holt Adoption Program processed approximately 370 Vietnamese children.[20]

. As a result of the North Vietnamese and Viet Cong military offensive in South Vietnam in March and April of 1975, and the collapse of the government in neighboring Cambodia, thousands of infants and children were abandoned by their families. The governments of the United States, Canada, England, and Australia airlifted approximately 1500 to 2000 orphaned Vietnamese and a smaller number of Cambodian children to their countries.

Of significance were the statements made by the receiving countries' governments to the effect that children destined for their respective shores were *not* those left parentless as a result of the March–April events. The children, they claimed, who were involved in the hurried evacuation from Vietnam and Cambodia were already in various phases of the adoptive process and were being cared for in accredited (Vietnamese) institutions operated primarily by the Holt Children Services and Friends of All Children. Many American families had been waiting 18 months for their children.[21] Contrary to what people, especially new potential adoptive couples thought, no additional children had been added to the population of adoptable children.

In other words, given the apparent chaotic conditions in many of its cities, the South Vietnamese government, always suspicious of intercountry adoptions, did not sanction an increase in the actual number of "exportable children." The receiving countries went to considerable length to emphasize that in no way did any child from Southeast Asia reach another country who would not in any event have arrived there. In light of the precarious situation, what the South Vietnamese Ministry of Social Affairs and the United States Bureau of Immigration and Naturalization would have people believe was that their role was an advocacy one expediting the children's departure and arrival, thereby reducing a six-month process to one week.[22]

Discrepancies existed, however, between what was officially announced and what actually occurred. For example, it was not uncommon for "orphans" to arrive without proper "papers" and subsequently to admit having living parents or relatives in Southeast Asia. Some were revealed as having been placed in orphanages only days before their departure from Vietnam. Others, children of VIPs, were accompanied on their flight by their mothers who posed as "aides."[23]

At an informal conference in Washington, D.C., sponsored by Congressman Paul E. Tsongas (Democrat, Massachusetts) regarding the evacuation of Vietnamese children, charges of racism and elitism were leveled against those who sought to adopt Vietnamese children. Many were accused of being on a "guilt trip." The feelings that surfaced at this meeting and the charges hurled at individuals and agencies fostering the intercountry transracial adoption of Oriental children, especially half-black, half-Vietnamese children, rekindled all the almost forgotten charges made against domestic transracial adoptions. "Do you think they'll be allowed in the South Boston schools?" one person asked. Another, a former employee of the Agency for International Development (AID), charged that many Vietnamese children had living parents and were being forcibly removed from their country against the wishes of their parents.[24] Some suggested that, in lieu of the massive airlifting of Vietnamese children to this country, the American government would be wiser to establish foster care programs in Vietñam and Cambodia.

In order to guard against unauthorized adoptions, a class action suit was filed by a group of California lawyers and by the Center of Constitutional Rights in New York, requesting that no adoption be made final until it could be established that the child in question was indeed an orphan.[25] In November 1975, a United States Court of Appeals ruled that the Immigration and Naturalization Service must allow access to its files to attorneys seeking to return Vietnamese children to their parents. The United Nations High Commissioner for Refugees, the International Red Cross, and the Children's Relief Fund promised to support the efforts of these attorneys in helping to locate the parents.[26]

Following the court's ruling controversy centered on the amount of information to be divulged to the Vietnamese authorities, the extent to which Vietnamese parents should be traced, and the possibility of reprisals being taken by the new Vietnamese government against parents who had sent their children to the United States.

One consequence of the suit was that the Immigration and Naturalization Service warned each adoptive couple in the United States that their Vietnamese child might not be legally eligible for adoption. By December 1975, the Immigration and Naturalization Service found that, at a minimum, 274 of the 1830 Vietnamese children airlifted to the United States during April 1975 were not eligible for adoption.[27]

In a somewhat related 1975 decision, a superior court in California ruled that Family Ministries, a sectarian adoption agency operating on behalf of World Vision, an evangelical Protestant organization, could no longer control the adoption of Cambodian children brought to the United States. The superior court justice argued that although most, if not all, of the children were Buddhists, only evangelical Protestant applicants were being considered by Family Ministries as adoptors. Jews, Catholics, Buddhists, and couples of no particular religion were excluded as prospective adoptive parents. "In cases where religion is unknown . . . the law merely requires adoption agencies to place a child in the home that is best able to meet his needs."[28]

One result, then, of the rapid evacuation of Vietnamese children to be eventually adopted by white American parents, was a replay of the original antitransracial adoption arguments, namely, that the act involved robbing a people of its most vital resource—its children.[29] Several black adoption agencies accused federal authorities of racism. They charged that Vietnamese children who had been fathered by black American military personnel (20,000 to 40,000 racially mixed children remain in South Vietnam) were not being matched with qualified black families.[30] Instead, they claimed, these children were being placed with white families. It is curious that, according to the above-mentioned agencies, black families were available for these children, more so than for native-born blacks eligible for adoption, many of whom are among the 100,000 to 125,000 children defined as hard to place.

At this point one has to consider the overall effects of the airlift on both race relations within the United States and the progress of domestic transracial adoption. While Americans can become extremely emotional about the plight of Vietnamese children (one commentator likened it to the emotionalism surrounding the return of the American POWs from Indochina), we continue to ignore a large pool of native-born black children who appear destined to live their lives in a series of foster homes or in institutions. Why, one continues to wonder, did all the major television evening news broadcasts and magazines display a telephone number where information concerning the adoption of Vietnamese children could be obtained and not allow "equal time" for American orphans needing homes? Why were 2000 Vietnamese children more worthy of front-page coverage [31] when the plight of thousands of homeless nonwhite children was only occasionally mentioned and then only on remote pages? "Why doesn't someone airlift children from Appalachia or Bedford-Stuyvesant? Those children belong in their country with their own people and culture," one person was quoted as saying.[32]

In reviewing the articles that appeared during the airlift of the Vietnamese children to this country, many people appeared to question the true motivation of this program. "The idea that it's to save children's lives angers me. It's the desire of families in this country who want children badly that has led to the airlift, not the likely death of the children, because that's unlikely," said George W. Webber, head of the New York Theological Seminary.[33] Caution was advised by leaders and professional employees of humanitarian agencies. In addition, one consistently found reference to guilt, guilt that many believe America was attempting to expiate by these adoptions.[34]

Politically, it was charged that the children were being manipulated by both the South Vietnamese and American governments for diplomatic ends. Both the International Red Cross and Caritas, the relief agency of the

Vatican, condemned the transfer of these children. Caritas called it "a deplorable and unjustifiable mistake,"[35] suggesting that Catholic agencies not be involved. The International Red Cross felt that this type of intercountry adoption was in violation of the section of the Geneva Convention that called for the education of war orphans within their own country.[36] Officially, however, the American government limited itself to two phases of the operation. It cut through the bureaucratic network, allowing for the rapid immigration of Vietnamese children to this country, and it provided transportation (huge C-5A cargo planes, one of which crashed, killing many Vietnamese children). In all other respects, it was the responsibility of private adoption agencies to see to it that the children were placed with adoptive families.

Some argued that the children were being sent to the United States at the behest of the American ambassador in Saigon, in hopes of arousing the sympathy of the American people so that they would prod Congress for actions considered favorable to the South Vietnamese (i.e., military aid). After the fall of South Vietnam, the new government officially requested that the United States return all the children *to their families* in South Vietnam.[37]

CONCLUDING COMMENTS

Initial attempts at intercountry adoption, especially from Asia, began the history of transracial adoption in the United States. They were the forerunners of transracial adoption as we recognize it today, involving native-born nonwhite children. Starting as an act of "Christian charity," by both individuals and agencies, intercountry adoptions were mistakenly viewed by some as an alternative to the dwindling supply of white children available for adoption. Reviewing the literature on either European and Oriental intercountry adoption, one is struck by the evangelical *qua* humanitarian nature of the individuals and organizations involved in this effort. The Holt Adoption Program, in particular, strongly emphasizes the importance of Christianity as essential to adoption. While a solution to childlessness certainly is the main agenda item of couples seeking an intercountry adoption, their additional motivation appears to be in rescuing (i.e., salvaging) a life.

Most early intercountry adoptions were for the most part achieved without the involvement of traditional adoption agencies. Consequently, the original organizations, guided basically by humanitarian motives, did not adhere to the policies established by professionals. Most early intercountry adoptions required only screening of potential parents by the contracting agency. Serious questions were raised by the social work profession regarding several aspects of the adoption procedure (e.g., the selection and investigation of potential parents, and continuing support services). By 1961, mainly through the efforts of the social work profession, legislation was enacted prohibiting proxy adoptions, forcing prospective adoptive parents to personally apply for and receive a child in the child's country of origin. The alternative was to allow a recognized (i.e., traditional) adoption agency to establish eligibility. At the present time, the accepted procedure for intercountry adoption is for the humanitarian agency to refer applications of potential adoptive parents' to a local professional agency, whereupon the preadoptive investigation begins, usually conducted by trained social workers. By 1975, most intercountry adoptions involved old-line social agencies.

In 1975, the CWLA, in a special report, supported the wisdom of preadoption services by recognized adoption agencies, indicating, however, that intercountry adoption served only a few children and was at best a difficult and at times frustrating procedure to endure.[38] The adoption of 2000 Vietnamese children notwithstanding, it does not appear that intercountry adoption will succeed as a viable alternative for childless couples seeking to adopt. The originating countries jealously guard their children as vital national resources, no matter how poor their situations are or how intolerable Americans would consider their living conditions.

Adoption, as defined by Western tradition, is in many of these countries a practice that has no real social or cultural precedent or support. The idea of adoption is often an anathema. This is especially true in the Orient where parentless children are not perceived so much as a societal responsibility as a responsibility that belongs to the extended family. The best that can be hoped for is not that these countries will be persuaded to increase their export of children, but that they will be helped to develop indigenous social services, including adoption. The latter is an institutional building process which is instilled slowly and is even more difficult to create. Nevertheless, as in the case of the Christian Adoption Program in Korea (CAPOK) the *threat* of adoption by others usually stimulated the development of local social services. In 1974, for example, Korea passed a law calling for the domestic adoption of a Korean child for every intercountry adoption.

Little systematic longitudinal investigation of intercountry adoption appears in the literature. What is found are either short-range follow-up studies or a limited number of case histories.[39] However, all the data now available concerning intercountry adoptions of Asian children indicate that they have made satisfactory adjustments.[40] For these intercountry transracial adoptions, as well as for domestic transracial adoptions, the crucial period is in the future. It still remains to be seen how these children will adjust during their adolescence and adulthood.

NOTES

1. In 1972 a group of American Indians issued the following statement concerning transracial adoption: "The identity crisis of adolescence is likely to be especially traumatic for the Indian child growing up in a White home. When they are old enough to realize that they're different there is likely to be real trouble, especially if White parents haven't made serious efforts to expose them to their own cultural heritage. . . . And trouble will come from the White family, too, they say. The White man's hatred of the native American may be forgotten when he's a cute helpless baby or child, but it will show up when the child becomes an adolescent and able to think and act as an individual," *Ann Arbor News* (July 17, 1972), p. 10.

2. President Lyndon B. Johnson, in a special message to Congress, March 3, 1968, referred to the American Indian as "the forgotten American."

3. Neither the National Center for Social Statistics nor HEW's Children's Bureau has a separate category for Indian adoptions.

4. Michael Shapiro, *A Study of Adoption Practices*, vol. 1: *Adoption Agencies and the Children They Serve*, Child Welfare League of America, New York, 1956, Chap. 7; Grace Gallay, "International Adoptions," *Canadian Welfare* Vol. 39, no. 6 (November–December, 1963), pp. 248–250; Donald E. Chambers, "Willingness to Adopt Atypical Children," *Child Welfare*, vol. 49, no. 5 (May 1970), pp. 275–279; Barbara P. Griffin and Marvin S. Arffa, "Recruiting Adoptive Homes for Minority Children—One Approach," *Child Welfare*, vol. 49, no. 2 (February 1970), pp. 105–107.

5. David Fanshel, *Far from the Reservation: The Transracial Adoption of American Indian Children*, Scarecrow Press, Metuchen, N.J., 1972.

6. Arnold Lyslo, "Adoption for American Indian Children," *Child Welfare*, vol. 39, no. 6 (June 1960), pp. 32–33; Arnold Lyslo, "Adoptive Placement of American Indian Children with Non-Indian Families, Part I—The Indian Project," *Child Welfare*, vol. 40, no. 5 (May 1961), pp. 4–6.

7. *Ibid.*

8. Arnold Lyslo, "The Indian Adoption Project—An Appeal to Catholic Charities to Participate," *Catholic Charities Review*, vol. 48, no. 5 (May 1964), pp. 12–16.

9. *Ibid.*

10. Arnold Lyslo, "Adoptive Placement of Indian Children," *Catholic Charities Review*, vol. 51, no. 2 (February 1967), pp. 23–25.

11. *Ibid.*

12. Fanshel, *op. cit.*, footnote 5, p. 280.

13. *Ibid.*, pp. 326, 328.

14. *Ibid.*, pp. 128, 179.

15. *Ibid.*, p. 339.

16. For example, *ARENA News*, Newsletter of the Adoption Resource Exchange of North America; *National Adoptalk*, National Council of Adoptive Organizations; *Opportunity*, A Division of the Boys and Girls Aid Society of Oregon.

17. Loren Jenkins, "Vietnam's War Torn Children," *Newsweek* (May 28, 1973), pp. 52–61.
18. U. S. Department of Justice, Immigration and Naturalization, "Immigrants Admitted to the U.S. by Country or Region of Birth, 1964–1973," Washington, D.C. (1974).
19. Edward B. Fiske, "Adopting Vietnam's Orphans: Efforts Grow to Make it Easier," *New York Times*, August 21, 1973, p. 24.
20. *Ibid.*
21. "Planeload of Vietnamese Orphans on Way to U.S.," *New York Times*, April 4, 1965, p. 1; James P. Sterba, "American Couples Beseige Agencies for Vietnamese Orphans," *New York Times*, April 3, 1975, p. 32.
22. "Saigon Adoptions Sped: 6 Month Job Cut to Week," *New York Times*, April 7, 1975, p. 20.
23. "Clouds over the Airlift," *Time* (April 28, 1975), p. 20.
24. Richard D. Lyons, "Washington Meeting on Children's Airlift Is Jarred by Charges of Racism and Elitism," *New York Times*, April 8, 1975, p. 14.
25. Douglas E. Kneeland, "U.S. to Review Refugee Orphan Status," *New York Times*, p. 21, May 9, 1975; "Suit Seeks to Block Adoption of Many Vietnamese Children," *New York Times*, May 1, 1975, p. 21.
26. "Refugee Adoption Still Unresolved," *New York Times*, November 9, 1975, p. 25.
27. "Battle for Custody of Vietnamese Children Is Stalled," *New York Times*, December 8, 1975, p. 16.
28. "Suit Seeks to Void a Refugee Ruling," *New York Times*, November 16, 1975, p. 28.
29. Fox Butterfield, "Orphans of Vietnam: One Last Agonizing Issue," *New York Times*, April 13, 1975, p. E3.
30. "Where They Go," *Time* (April 14, 1975), p. 14.
31. Nancy Hicks, "Black Agencies Charge Injustice in Placing of Vietnam Children," *New York Times*, April 19, 1975, p. 11.
32. Shawn G. Kennedy, "Humanitarian, Say Some; Easing Guilt, Say Others," *New York Times*, April 9, 1975, p. 48.
33. Richard Flaste, "High Aide Says U.S. May Airlift 3,000 More Refugee Youngsters: Controversy Is Growing," *New York Times*, April 9, 1975, p. 1.
34. "The Orphans: Saved or Lost?" *Time* (April 21, 1975), p. 13.
35. *Ibid.*
36. Malcolm W. Browne, "Opposition Charge Denied," *New York Times*, April 8, 1975, p. 14; "U.S. Envoy in Saigon Is Quoted on Propaganda Effect of Airlift," *New York Times*, April 7, 1975, p. 20; Butterfield, *op. cit.*, footnote 29.
37. "Saigon Is Said to Demand Refugee Children Return," *New York Times*, May 10, 1975, p. 11.
38. "Special Report from Child Welfare League of America," *Child Welfare* Vol. LIV, no. 1 (January 1975), pp. 54–55.
39. John E. Adams and Hyung Bok Kim, "A Fresh Look at Intercountry Adoptions," *Children*, Vol. 18, no. 6 (November–December 1971), pp. 214–221.
40. Winthrop A. Rockwell, "Efforts Grow to Bring Here Babies that G.I.'s Left in Vietnam," *New York Times*, January 2, 1972, p. 22; Lloyd B. Graham, "Children from Japan in American Adoptive Homes," *Casework Papers* (1957), pp. 130–145; Robert E. McDermott, "Oriental Adoptive Placements," *Catholic Charities Review* (April 1965), pp. 24–25; Letita Di Virgilio, "Adjustment of Foreign Children in Their Adoptive Homes," *Child Welfare*, Vol. 35, no. 9 (November 1956), pp. 15–21.

SECTION TWO

FIELD RESEARCH
ON TRANSRACIAL ADOPTION

The three chapters in this section are the heart of the book. They report the results of a survey of 204 white families who adopted at least one nonwhite child. The survey's respondents were the parents, the adopted children, and all the white siblings, whose ages ranged from three to eight. The children's interviews focused on racial awareness, attitudes, and identity. Each of these concepts was measured by projective techniques. Chapter 5 reviews prior studies of children's racial attitudes, but none of these studies had adopted children as respondents. Chapter 4, which focuses on the parents, describes their motivations for adopting the child they did, the changes the adopted child introduced into their lives, their perceptions of their adopted child and their other children's adjustment to each other, and their expectations and hopes about the future racial identity and adjustment of their adopted child. Our study, unlike Fanshel's and Grow and Shapiro's, which are referred to in Section One, relies as much on the children's responses as it does on those of the parents. For this reason, it provides the reader with more direct, first-hand information about the adjustments involved in multiracial families than other studies of families who adopted transracially.

CHAPTER **FOUR**

A SOCIAL PROFILE
OF WHITE FAMILIES
WHO ADOPTED TRANSRACIALLY

This chapter provides a composite of the 204 families in our survey who adopted nonwhite children. It describes their socioeconomic characteristics and their perceptions of the changes that have occurred within their families, as well as the reactions of relatives, neighbors, and friends to their decision. It also examines the parents' motivations for adopting the child they did, as well as their expectations about their children's and their own racial identity and preferences over time. Where appropriate, the characteristics of our respondents are compared to those described in other surveys of families who have adopted transracially.

Since the interviews we conducted were limited to five states, all of which are located in the Midwest, we could not be sure that our findings could be generalized to families on the East and West Coasts who have also adopted transracially. But all the data we have seen since completing our survey indicate that the profile based on our families can be generalized to other parts of the country.

SOCIOECONOMIC CHARACTERISTICS

In analyzing the mothers' and fathers' responses to questions concerning the amount of schooling they have had, the job they hold, the family's income, and the political party they support, one cannot help but be struck by the seeming homogeneity of the families' social and economic status. Their educational backgrounds, for example, show that at least 62 percent of the mothers completed four years of college and 28 percent of them continued on to graduate school (Table 4.1). The table also shows that 61 percent of the fathers attended university past the bachelor's degree. Sixty-eight percent of the fathers work as professionals. Most of them are ministers, social workers, or academicians. Among the remaining third, 12 percent are businessmen, and the other 20 percent are clerical workers, salesmen, skilled laborers, or graduate students.

None of the mothers holds a full-time job outside the home. Almost all of them explained that when they and their husbands made the decision to adopt it also involved a commitment on the wife's part to remain at home in the role of full-time mother. Before they were married, or before they adopted their first child, 46 percent of the mothers held jobs in a profes-

TABLE 4.1 Mothers' and fathers' education

Highest Number of Years of Schooling	Mother	Father
	(In Percent)	
High School Only	13	5
1-3 years College	25	16
4 years of College	34	18
Post-Graduate Study	28	61

sional capacity, and 3 percent were enrolled as graduate students. About 14 percent did not work outside the home before they gave birth to, or adopted, their first child.

The parents were shown a list of annual income categories and asked to place themselves in the appropriate one. The income distribution shown in Table 4.2 clearly places all the families in what is considered the middle class.

If, however, one were to predict the incomes of these families on the basis of the educational attainments of the male respondents, it is quite likely that one would predict heavier representation in the $25,000 and above" category. The fact that 68 percent of the fathers work in professional occupations would also lead one to expect incomes higher than these shown in Table 4.2. But observing that a majority of the fathers have chosen such traditionally low-paying professions as the ministry, social work, youth work, and teaching, one can better understand the lack of status congruity represented by high occupational and educational achievement and relatively low income.

The Midwest is heavily Protestant; and so are the respondents in our sample. Sixty-three percent of the mothers and 57 percent of the fathers acknowledged belonging to some Protestant congregation. Lutheranism was

TABLE 4.2 Distribution of annual family income

Annual Income	Percentage of Respondents
$ 5,000 - 9,999	7
10,000 - 14,999	34
15,000 - 19,000	32
20,000 - 24,999	14
25,000 and over	13
No answer	1
Total	100

cited by 19 percent of both mothers and fathers. Twenty-one and 22 percent of the parents are Catholics (which is commensurate with the national Catholic representation); 1 and 2 percent are Jewish (at least 50 percent less than the national representation), and the remaining 15 and 19 percent acknowledged no formal religious identification or affiliation. Most of the parents who acknowledged a religious affiliation also said they attended church regularly, as the figures in Table 4.3 indicate.

The church seems to play an important role in the lives of many of these families. Some have reported that much of their social life is organized around their church, and that their friends usually belong to it too, especially other families who have adopted nonwhite children. One of the families cited their affiliation with the church as the major factor in their decision to adopt. Mrs. J. explained her feelings this way: "I think when you are involved, when you consider yourself a Christian and are involved in an interracial congregation it's silly for a person to preach something and not to do that themselves."

Another couple, a family with an income of over $50,000 a year, described the church as the center of much of the social service activities in which the wife is engaged. Through their church, both parents have become involved in an inner-city housing program and have met and made friends with black families. The husband described their life-style this way:

Our whole lifestyle in the last several years has changed considerably. The church, and our working in the housing program, has really made us more aware of racial problems. The natural social climate of people like ourselves in the society is mostly

TABLE 4.3 Frequency of church attendance

Frequency	Mothers	Fathers
	(In Percent)	
At least once a week	50	47
A few times per month	17	14
A few times a year	13	13
Not at all	18	21
Other, No Answer	2	3

one of skiing and hunting and fishing and the arts and parties. It is a rather superficial style of life, in large part, I think, because doctors by and large see so many problems in their work that they are not overly fond of coming home from death and dying to see more problems. So they are attracted to a social climate of nondescript playing. We have kind of gotten out of this sort of social climate. Through the work with our church we have become aware of other problems. We've met other people in the church who seem more real. Once you start spending a lot of your time discussing problems of your country, the world, your city, race, it's a little difficult to stand around and talk about a skiing trip.

Political affiliations and activities are not as involving as the church for most of the families. About a third of the parents described themselves as independent, about 40 percent as Democrats, and 12 percent as Republicans; the others had no preference or named a local party (in Minnesota it was the Farmer Labor Party) as the one they generally supported or had voted for in the last election. Only a small proportion, less than a quarter of the group, said that they belonged to a local political club or that they worked for a political candidate.

One final comment about the social characteristics of these families: 78 percent reported that the neighborhood in which they live is all white. Four percent characterized it as predominately black; and the other 18 percent said they lived in a mixed neighborhood. Among the large majority who lived in an all-white neighborhood, only a few talked about this as being inappropriate to their life-style since the adoption. A few were making plans to move. But most of the parents did not find the homogeneity of the neighborhood in which they lived a disturbing or incongruous factor.

The socioeconomic characteristics of the families in our study closely matched those reported by Grow and Shapiro.[1] Although Grow and Shapiro's families were distributed across all regions of the United States, they found, as we did, that the parents were better educated than average (a majority of the fathers had attended university past the bachelor's degree, and about half of the mothers had attended college for at least four years). Over half of the fathers held professional or technical positions. They also found that about two-thirds of the families were Protestant and that most of the parents were regular churchgoers. Religion played an important part in the lives of the families in the Grow and Shapiro sample, as it did in ours. Many of their respondents, like ours, traced their motivation for adopting a nonwhite child to their religious beliefs and church affiliation.

In both samples, the parents thought of themselves as liberals or independent, but with few exceptions (10 and 4 percent respectively), the families live in all-white or predominantly white neighborhoods. In other words, although in both surveys the parents claimed to be more liberal in their political views or affiliations than their socioeconomic status might lead one to predict, their choice of where to live was quite consistent with their status as middle-class, educated, professional people.

DEMOGRAPHIC CHARACTERISTICS

The parents ranged in age from 25 to 50. The average age of the mother was 34 and that of the father 36.[2] They had been married for an average of 12 years; the shortest time was 2 years and the longest was 25 years.

The number of children per family ranged from one to nine (this includes natural children as well as adopted children). Nineteen percent of the parents did not have any natural children (all those in this category described themselves as unable to bear children). The range of children born and adopted in all the families is shown in Table 4.4.[3]

The families who adopted more than three children were in almost all instances ones in which the father or both parents were professionally involved in adoption services, youth work, or social work. They had had prior experience as foster parents, and some had foster children currently living with them. In a sense, their decision to adopt and their plans to make themselves available as foster parents were part of their professional roles.

Twenty-six percent of the families had adopted their first child. Since 19 percent of these parents were unable to bear children, it turns out that only 7 percent of those who had children born to them had adopted their first child. In many cases, the fact that parents who were not infertile had had children born to them before they adopted was not a matter of choice, but a reflection of the policy of the adoption agency with which they were dealing. Unless a couple could produce medical evidence that they were unable to bear a child, most of them were "strongly advised" to have at least one child; and then, if they were still interested in adoption, the agency would be willing to consider their candidacy.

The ordinal position of the first adopted child in these families is shown in Table 4.5. Among those families who adopted more than one child (56 percent) the second adopted child occupied the "middle" position 35 percent of the time and the "youngest" position 65 percent of the time.[4]

The distribution by racial characteristics of the first and second adopted children is shown in Table 4.6. American blacks make up the largest

TABLE 4.4 Total number of children, number adopted, and number born into families

Total Number of Children	Percentage of Families		No. of Children Adopted	No. of Children Born into Family
1	3	3	1	-
2	16		1	1
		26		
2	10		2	-
3	2		3	-
3	6	26	2	1
3	18		1	2
4	3		4	-
4	2		3	1
		24		
4	9		2	2
4	10		2	2
5	1		5	-
5	1		4	1
5	1	11	3	2
5	4		2	3
5	4		1	4
6	1		4	2
6	1	4	2	4
6	2		1	5
7	2		4	3
7	1	5	2	5
7	1		1	6

TABLE 4.5 Ordinal position of first adopted child

Position	Percent
Oldest	26[a]
Middle	32
Youngest	41

[a]In 73 percent of these families, there were no children born to the parents

TABLE 4.6 Racial characteristics of first and second adopted children

Characteristics[a]	First Adoption	Second Adoption
	(In Percent)	
American black	65	70
American Indian	11	3
Korean	5	9
Mexican/Puerto Rican	5	1
White	14	17
Total	100	100

[a]Forty-four percent of the parents described their children as mixed-- Negro and White--and 17 percent described them as a combination of American Negro, American Indian, and Mexican.

category of adopted children. They comprise the category of children who are the most available for adoption.[5] Most of the families wanted a racially mixed child, but they did not have strong preferences concerning the specific characteristics of the mixture. Some of the families, but fewer than 10, said they felt that the problems of adopting a black child would be more than they were willing or able to undertake.[6] One family said: "At the time we weren't ready to adopt a black child. Taking an Indian child was less of a step."

Another family said about their experience with adoption, "I was afraid of what my parents and other people would say. But I've changed and by the time we adopted our second child, I only wanted a Negro child."

Comments such as these came from parents who adopted Korean or American Indian children. But more typical responses were ones such as the following:

We wanted more children than two. We started worrying about the population explosion. We knew that there was not much of a possibility of our adopting a white child. We felt that we could handle a child that maybe some other people could not. We knew that there was a need for parents who would adopt a racially mixed child. Once we decided to adopt we discussed who we would like to adopt and we both agreed that we'd like to adopt a minority child. I think part of the reason was that we had both spent two years in Africa in the Peace Corps. Seeing all these differences in people was interesting and exciting and not threatening. And we wanted to, if we could, incorporate those differences into our family. So we decided we would take a minority child and we weren't really specific as to what kind. We didn't think in terms of a black child or Indian child. We just thought whoever needed a home we would take. At the time the hardest to place child was the black child, and so since we had been in Africa, that was no problem with us. We had some black friends with whom we were fairly close and we decided that was fine. We wanted any mixed race, Negro or Indian, any mixed race. We told the agency it made no difference as long as she is brown.

One of the families who adopted a black child felt that they had been propagandized and given misinformation by the adoption agency. Mrs. G. said:

We were all naive about our racial feelings. We wanted to do good works. We had all this input from agencies who said that no black families would adopt. We gained the impression that the children would stay in institutions for the rest of their lives. We believed that these agencies knew the truth and were telling it to us. Since we wanted to have a different kind of family, one with all kinds of people in it and since we thought we could provide a good home and since we were interested in black people and black culture and since we had a feeling that we wanted to know more about black people and what their struggle was, we went about with the adoption.

Mr. and Mrs. G. felt that the agencies had deceived them, and that indeed, there are black parents who want to adopt black children. In their words: "We feel now that if a black child can find a black home that is the ideal. If we were to adopt today, knowing what we know about the interest and availability of black parents, we would not adopt a black child and we would not help or advise anyone else to do it."

Among those families who adopted one child, 56 percent adopted a boy and 44 percent a girl. Among those families who adopted more than one child, 60 percent adopted boys and girls, 22 percent adopted only boys, and 18 percent adopted only girls. The sex ratio for all the adopted children shows that 41 percent of the families adopted only a boy, 32 percent adopted only a girl, and 27 percent adopted both sexes. The overall pattern thus reveals a slight preference for boys over girls. In almost every instance, when parents expressed a preference for a boy or girl, it was because they wanted a child to match or complement a desired family pattern. For some, a girl was needed as a sister, or a boy was wanted as a brother; for others, there were only boys in the family and the parents wanted a daughter, or vice versa. In only a few instances did childless parents indicate that they had had a sex preference.

The ages at which the first and second children were adopted are shown in Table 4.7. Note that 69 percent of the first-child adoptions were of children less than one year of age compared to 80 percent of the second-child adoptions. One explanation for the greater proportion of younger adoptions the second time around is that adoption agencies were more likely to provide families who had already proven themselves, by their successful first adoption, with their most desirable and sought after children than they were to place such children in untried homes.

In summary, the demographic characteristics show that on the average families had between three and four children. Forty-four percent adopted one child, and 41 percent adopted two children. The large majority adopted after they had had at least one child (although not necessarily as a matter of choice). Black children were adopted by at least two-thirds of the families, followed by American Indian, Korean, white, and Mexican or Puerto Rican children. When a family adopted one child, there was a slightly greater likelihood that it would be a boy; but when more than one child was adopted, 60 percent adopted both a boy and a girl. About 70 percent of the

TABLE 4.7 Ages of children at first and second adoption

Ages	First Adoption	Second Adoption [•]
	(In Percent)	
Less than 1 month	11	11
1 to 2 months	27	24
3 to 5 months	13	28
6 to 11 months	18	17
1 year to 1 year 11 months	11	10
2 years to 2 years 11 months	3	1
3 years to 4 years 11 months	6	2
5 years and older	8	7
No Answer	2	–

first adoptions and 80 percent of the second adoptions were babies less than one year old.[7]

IDEAS AND BELIEFS ABOUT ADOPTION

The next part of the interview shifted from soliciting descriptive information to inquiring about the attitudes and beliefs the respondents held about adoption at the time they were considering adopting their first child. Twenty-four percent said they reached their decision to adopt after they realized that they could not bear children and because they were convinced that they wanted to have a family.[8] Thirty-eight percent of the respondents in the Grow and Shapiro survey expressed similar feelings. Eight percent said they decided to adopt their first child after they had borne all the children they planned to bear and these children were adolescents or older. Forty percent said that the decision to adopt was a combination of the following reasons: an interest in adoption that extended back into their own childhood and that arose out of a strong desire to provide a home for hard-to-adopt children, and a belief that adoption was a more moral way of having children than bearing them, given the pressures of overpopulation. Many of the parents who emphasized their interest in adopting a hard-to-place child explained that the contacts they had as a result of the work they were involved in made them especially sensitive to the need for providing good homes for such children. In the Grow and Shapiro survey, 28 percent said they were specifically interested in transracial adoptions. Fifty-four percent of the parents expressed comparable beliefs.

The average length of time that had elapsed between the parents' decision to adopt and their obtaining their first child was seven years, four months. Thirty-one percent of the parents said that they began contacting adoption agencies within five years after they were married.

Most of the families described good working relations with the adoption agency. Several commented on how much easier it was and how much less time was involved in obtaining a second child than a first. A few recounted stories of being pleasantly surprised when their social worker contacted them shortly (less than a year) after they had received their first child and asked if they were interested in another. A few of the parents, however, felt bitter toward a particular social worker or agency because of the amount of time involved, or because of the agency's insistence that the couple come back after they had had a child, or because of the quality of the advice or information they provided about the type of child that was available or that they ought to adopt.[9]

One family felt that the adoption agency worked too quickly. They described a family who had gone to an agency "when they weren't certain about their feelings toward transracial adoption. In two weeks a child had been placed in their home and they weren't really ready for that child. The mother told me herself she had a lot of guilt feelings toward him and she felt she didn't love him as much as her own. It happened too fast for them; and they really didn't think about it enough."

A consistent comment made by parents who adopted older children concerned the lack of information they had received from the social worker about the child. One family who had adopted several children over 12 months of age and who were very active in the Open Door Society put it bluntly: "I don't think the agencies often know very much about the kids. I don't trust the worker's judgment at all. They don't know whether the child is slow or retarded or normal or anything." Another parent explained that they had received important information about how their adopted child had been treated by his foster mother from a friend—information they thought the caseworker should have given them.

We asked the parents about other types of children that they would or would not have accepted for their first adoption if they had not obtained the child they did. The characteristics discussed were: mental retardation, physical handicaps, age, sex, and race. A mentally retarded child was unacceptable to more of the parents than any other type. Two-thirds of the parents felt that they could and would not have accepted such a child. An additional 6 percent said that they had never considered a mentally retarded child when they were planning to adopt; and an additional 10 percent said they had considered it and would have accepted such a child only if the retardation were not severe. They discussed the difficulties such a child would pose with regard to other children in the family and to themselves as well. Many of the parents described themselves and their family as being "verbal," "articulate," and "quick." The mothers, especially, said they thought they would not have the patience or the time they believed would be required to cope with a mentally retarded child. Only 1 percent said, unequivocally, they would accept a mentally retarded child. In addition, most of the families also explained that they did not have the financial resources to undertake the care of such a child.

A smaller proportion, 39 percent, said that they would not have adopted a child with a physical handicap. Four percent said they had never considered such a child; 10 percent said they would have adopted a child with a physical handicap if he or she were not totally disabled; and 25 percent said they would have adopted such a child if the handicap were correctable at a moderate expense. Most of the parents who ruled out adoption of a physically handicapped child did so because of the expense they imagined would be involved in taking care of such a child. Eight percent said unequivocally they would have adopted a child with a physical handicap if they could not have obtained the child they did.

These preferences with regard to the mentally and physically handicapped suggest that the availability of a pool of "white middle-class professional" potential adoptive parents for one type of hard-to-place child does not apply to all categories of hard-to-place children. Given the characteristics of our sample frame, it is not possible to estimate whether there are more parents who are willing and anxious to adopt a nonwhite hard-to-place child than there are parents who are willing to adopt a physically and mentally handicapped hard-to-place child. But our data do allow the conclusion that, for those children who are hard to place in more than one respect, the chances of finding receptive parents must be extremely slim.

Age and sex are characteristics about which few of the parents had set preferences. For example, about half said they had no preference concerning the child's sex; 28 percent said they would have accepted only a boy, and 24 percent said they would have accepted only a girl. Practically all the parents who said they did have a preference about the sex of their adopted child based that preference on the fact that they already had a child of the opposite sex, or of the same sex, and wanted the adopted child to match or complement the child already in the family. Only 6 percent of the parents who did not have any children prior to the adoption expressed preferences about the sex of the child they wanted to adopt.

More of the parents exhibited preferences about the age of the child they wanted to adopt than about the child's sex. Only 8 percent said that age was not a factor at all. Forty-one percent would have accepted only a baby up to one year of age, 20 percent up to two years, and 14 percent up to five years of age.[10] The others mentioned ages that would have meshed with children already in the family; for example, the child should be younger than the oldest child, or older than the youngest.

When the parents were asked about their preferences for children of other races (i.e., other than the race of the child they adopted), 54 percent said they would have accepted a child in any racial category (including white), 17 percent said any category except white, 5 percent said any category except black, and 9 percent said they would have accepted a child only from the category from which they had obtained one.

Parents who adopted Korean children said that they thought they and the children would have an easier time than families who adopted black children. One of the families who adopted an eleven-year-old Korean girl discussed the feasibility of her returning to Korea when she becomes an adult. The child has an aunt and uncle in Korea with whom she has remained in contact.

The responses cited above show that at least 54 percent of the parents wanted to adopt a healthy, normal baby and that the adoption of a black, Indian, or Korean child was not the major criterion. In most instances they accepted and were happy with a nonwhite baby because they were able to obtain the child more quickly than they could have obtained a white child who met their health, age, and sex requirements. Seventeen percent had made up their minds at the outset that they would not adopt a white child, and 5 percent had decided that they would adopt a nonwhite child so long as he or she was not black. Thus only a minority of the parents had decided prior to the adoption that they would accept only a nonwhite child. For the majority, other criteria, the most prominent of which were the physical and mental health of the child, were the determining factors in their decision to adopt a particular child.

We established two categories of parents: those who were unable to bear children, and those who were interested only in transracial adoption; and we compared the attitudes expressed by each about the type of child they would have accepted if they had not been able to obtain the child they did. Sixty-six percent of the parents who could not bear children, and 81 percent of those who wanted to adopt only transracially, said they would not have accepted a mentally retarded child. Thirty-nine and 44 percent would not have accepted a child with a severe physical handicap. Thirty-five and 38 percent would have considered a child with a physical handicap if the handicap were correctable at a reasonable cost.

Age and sex were factors about which the parents in the two categories disagreed. Fifty-four percent of the parents who could not bear children said they would not have accepted a child more than one year of age, compared to 34 percent of the parents who wanted to adopt a nonwhite child. Fifty-eight percent of the parents who could not bear children said the sex of the child was not important, compared to 45 percent of the parents who wanted to adopt transracially. All the preferences are summarized in Table 4.8.

Parents who stipulated at the outset that they wished to adopt only a nonwhite child were more discriminating about the type of child they were willing to accept than were parents who could not bear children. The latter of course had fewer options available to them.

Several families who had already adopted their first nonwhite child discussed the importance they attached to adopting a second nonwhite child. One father put it this way: "We feel it is important that S not be the only minority child in a white family. He needs someone within the family of his own race to identify with. I think it's very important for him to be able to say he's not the only brown-skinned child in the family. He thinks it is important too. He's very excited about it. He says, 'She's going to be adopted like me, and she's even going to be brown like me.' So it's tremendous for him."

In general our findings about the children's characteristics that the families found most desirable or that they were willing to accept were similar to those reported by Grow and Shapiro, who concluded their discussion of this issue as follows.

TABLE 4.8 Characteristics of children who would not have been acceptable for first adoption, by parents who could not bear children and by parents who wanted to adopt only nonwhite children

Type of Child Would Not Have Accepted	Parents Who Could Not Bear Children	Parents Who Wanted to Adopt Only Non-white Children
	(In Percent)[a]	
Mentally retarded	66	81
Physically handicapped	39	44
Correctably physically handicapped	35	38
Boy	20	31
Girl	22	24
Older than one year	46	66
Total N	48	58

[a]The percentages are not supposed to total 100. Each category represents the percentage who answered "unacceptable"; the figures that do not appear on the table are the percentage who would have accepted a child in that category.

Many had not sought a black child initially, but concern about the needs of black children coupled with unavailability of healthy white children led them to this decision. They had some reservations about this most often because of their families' attitude or because they were not sure a black child would be happy with white parents.

These parents would have been willing to consider a child of almost any racial background, but many would have had serious reservations about adopting a child over eight years old or one with intellectual or physical handicaps.[11]

RELATIONS AMONG FAMILY MEMBERS, OTHER RELATIVES, FRIENDS, AND NEIGHBORS

A new addition to a family, no matter how carefully planned for ahead of time and no matter how much he or she is desired, is likely to bring about changes in familial and interpersonal relations. When the new addition is an adopted child of another race, the ramifications are likely to be even greater and to affect relations beyond the nuclear family. Grandparents, aunts, uncles, cousins, friends, and neighbors may alter their relationships with all the members of the family.

We asked the parents whether changes or problems were experienced by the family as a result of the adoption, and about the nature of these experiences. We asked about problems that they might currently be having or that they had had earlier in their relations with the adopted child involving the adopted child and his or her siblings, and involving themselves and the child or children born to them.

Sixty-two percent of the parents said that they were not presently experiencing difficulties or having problems with their adopted child. Initially, for the first few weeks, a large proportion of those who had become parents for the first time claimed that they had had some difficulties adjusting to their new roles. But they felt that they would have had to make the same adjustments if the child had been born to them and/or if the child had been white.

There is a relationship, however, between the race of the adopted child and the proportion of parents who acknowledged that they had had difficulties with the child. For example, 18 percent of the parents who had adopted a white child as their first adopted child said that they had had problems with him or her, in contrast to 39 and 47 percent of the parents who had adopted black and Indian or Asian children, respectively. But among all three categories, the explanation most often given for the difficulties was problems had developed as a result of the foster care the child had received prior to the adoption and not because of the child's race.

One of the families had an extraordinary story to tell about their experiences with a seven-year-old American Indian child they had adopted five years prior to the interview. It is the only family in our sample who had a tragic or near tragic experience resulting from the decision to adopt. Both parents have graduate degrees. They had one child prior to the adoption, who was a year older than C, the adopted girl. After adopting C the mother gave birth to two other children. They had tried to adopt a child before their first child was born. Their only requirement was that the child be healthy; the child's age, sex, and race were relatively unimportant. The agency with whom they were dealing put them off by urging them to wait until they had been married longer, and until, if possible, they could bear a child. The couple went back after their first child was born and indicated that they still wished to adopt a child. By this time they were quite sure they wanted a nonwhite child. A two-year-old American Indian girl was available. The parents were delighted, and the child was placed in their home. At the time of the adoption the parents did not know, and it is not clear from their story whether or not the social worker knew, that C was suffering from phenyl-ketonuria (PKU).[12] The parents described the following events which occurred shortly after C came into their home.

For the first day and night she just did not cry. She did not show any remorse at all for her foster parents. We were expecting a week of crying and were braced for it, but she was so angry that she couldn't be broken up. She didn't seem to know how to play with children. She followed G (her 3½ year old brother) around bugging him. We protected her from G bashing her, but instead began bashing her ourselves. She had had a hard time. She started screaming out of nowhere. We put the lid on that. Then she started wetting her pants; we could stop one, but the other would erupt in a scene. She started nursery school at the age of three, but she was disruptive. She demanded that the "Mother" hold her. She screamed, pushed, would not play with other children and would not sit and listen.

She very early learned how to con adults. She had the habit of sitting in the hospital and pressing the button and having someone come running. She tends to play that game with adults in terms of disruptive behavior. Fortunately the teachers at the nursery school keyed into that, as we did. You can't ignore it. She was there two years disrupting the place, then she went into kindergarten, and they were calling us to come and get her. They said she was screaming and wandering around the class, disrupting everything. We finally had her examined and referred to the Children's Psychiatric Clinic. She's been an outpatient at the clinic now for two years. They also put her on medication when she was in kindergarten which helps, a little. She also had a real good way of dividing us. We were ready for a divorce. We were all screaming and fighting with each other and would wind up beating up on her. It's really amazing how you can start out with good intentions and end up with such a mess.

None of the girls in the neighborhood, well, with the exception of one, will play with her. She's had trouble competing with G (her older brother). He's very bright and very likeable and has lots of friends and she's terribly jealous of him. Then the baby (D) came along six months after we adopted her. I guess she's terribly jealous of D. According to her psychiatrist it was to the point of slashing pictures and tearing up clothing. She had a period a year ago where she just wrecked up everything D had.

Anything D got, if she didn't have the same thing, she wrecked it. She's gotten over some of it. D of course came into the house with her here, and as a small baby. She's very active and very silly, and it is really easy to relate to her. So that D still has a pretty good relationship with her. But she has been asking more and more questions about her. D tends to put most of the blame on adoption; the kids all make comments like, "I came from my mommy's tummy and you didn't" which does not help. I suppose it's normal in a situation like this where there are so few adopted children. She has a lot of strikes against her, because she's at a point where, emotionally, she can't keep up with the four year olds. She's really had to push herself the past year to stay ahead of D.

I think there's basically a good deal of loyalty between D and G and they are both getting more and more tired of her. He is finding himself harassed by her. She's going through a stage right now where she's just obsessed with swear words, "screw me," "fuck you," "all that shit" and all that stuff. He eggs her on, but then he gets it back. G keys in to the fact that she makes us angry, so he tries to make us happy about him, then he makes her make us angry. It's really complicated.

In response to the question about problems involving the parents and the other children in the family stemming from the adoption, C's parents went on as follows:

Well everything is so complex because of her behavior problems that we can't tell. G blames the PKU rather than the adoption. He says she acts bad because she has PKU. G has had some really severe times when he's wanted her to go back. G gets really upset. Also, we've tried to maintain the same standards for her as with G. And we've been very strict with G and we felt we had to be strict with her. We did feel that we had to let up on her because she's not functioning as a seven year old, she's functioning as a four year old, or even a two year old, and it's difficult for him to accept this and some of this is due to the adoption. It's all so complicated.

The question is, If she had been a natural child would this have happened? We have no basis of knowing whether if she'd been born into the family, even if she had come in as an infant and been exactly as she is, how G would have regarded her. C has been the scapegoat almost since the beginning. G plays palsy-walsy with D. He says we're pals because we're the same color, because we both came out of mommy's tummy, and we're not adopted. He may not say it in exactly those words, but it has the same meaning. You can almost hear him say it.

On family relations, friends, and neighbors they provided the following account.

At first my family [the mother's] supported it. Then in the past several years, we've had quite a bit of trouble with the kids and my parents have gotten more and more discouraged. Last summer they indicated quite strongly that they felt we should take

C back. There was some feeling on the part of the social worker that we might be able to make other arrangements. We had gone through a period of feeling that it was not working out. Then this summer we went to visit his mother and she hadn't seen us since D was a year. We had indicated that we didn't want to stay with her because we'd been having trouble with the family. But she finagled around and we ended up staying with her and then we did have quite a scene. So then she told us she's never supported it and we should give her back. She had sort of waited to see how it was working out and now that it was not working out she's against it. His [the father's] brothers are quite supportive. My sister lives in Japan, and we only see her overnight about once every four years. She's sorry we're not getting along.

We moved here after we had had C about a year. The neighbors have been quite supportive and very nice to her, and most of them accepting. They have occasionally set limits, one neighbor wouldn't let her on her porch because she screamed so much. Another finally wouldn't let her anywhere in the house except in the basement because she peed in the bed so much, but they still were quite supportive. No one invites her to their home, I think the neighbors got tired of the screaming. They don't invite her to go anywhere.

If she had turned out to be a normal child . . . we told the social worker that we have three children who turned out to be pretty much normal, so we don't think it's us. We don't think we created a monster. (Mother) I think I've become much more angry, I feel I'm angry all the time. (Father) We certainly are more jumpy. (Mother) I think we're very pessimistic. We find it very difficult to go to COAC meetings because we're so pessimistic about adoption. I talked to a couple of girls at church last night and I warned them about getting older children. They're looking for Vietnamese children. We told the social worker at the very beginning we didn't think we could cope with a child with emotional problems or one who was dull or hard to teach, or hard to learn. That was one condition we put down. It turns out that that's what we got—what we didn't want. We don't suffer the guilt problems, necessarily, but we are feeling very sad about the whole business, and finding it hard to be in public.

Of course, this account is extraordinary. The more typical problems parents related about their initial interactions with the adopted child appear in excerpts such as the following.

He had been in a foster home in Florida in a black home in a ghetto situation. He could only count to three when we got him at age 4½, so one immediate problem we had was getting him ready for kindergarten next fall. And we put most of our efforts into preparing him because he's a very sharp little boy. He catches on very fast. But, for example, he had never put a puzzle together, never colored with crayons. The average child automatically does this with no questions asked. He's never experienced any of these things so that was one big problem, preparing him to face a school situation, to be on top of the situation. He'll be the top of his class, I'll guarantee it. We're still working on discipline. We'll probably be for a long, long while. In his foster home he was the favorite of three foster children. All the same age, all boys. He was favored because he was the light-skinned child out of three Negro children in a Negro home. There was no father in the home. Just a mother in her sixties and P was spoiled rotten. Anything other than monetary things, he had. Until she could not tolerate it any more, then she beat him. And to him this means love. And so this is the only type of discipline he's known, complete unruliness until wham the lid comes down and you spank him. And so we've had trouble with him, adjusting to our form of discipline. We've been using Rudolf Driekurs' form of discipline and it's hard for him to cope with. He'll push to the point of spanking him. Little by little we are withdrawing the physical punishment but this is very necessary for him. He will admit it. He wants me to spank him because, he will tell me, it means I love him and I care for him. We've had a problem of bed-wetting. He's been wet a whole year. He'll tell you if you ask, yes, he wets the bed to get even with us for taking him away from his foster home. He's a smart child and he knows why his behavior is as it is. But he is unable to correct it.

□ ■ □ ■

M has one panic point, and you saw it just now. When a stranger comes she thinks she's going to be moved. And she hasn't been moved since she was two when we saw her standing there. Especially if she goes into another room that has other children standing around, she thinks, "Oh boy, here I go." She was moved four times before we got her. And so when she sees a bunch of authority-looking figures with briefcases come into the room and look her over she panics. That's one thing. Another thing was it took her a little while to break into the rules of the house. Every now and then she would go right ahead and do something and we'd bring it to her attention. And then she would do something and be surprised no one would say anything—something about the rules of the house where she was before. So it took her a little while.

□ ■ □ ■

P came at the age of one. And I don't know how to describe it. She was something like a vegetable. She was not a normal type of child. She was extremely anemic, frequently had bronchitis, and did not respond. She just sat on the floor and pounded her head against the wall or against her bed. I had thought that part of it was her adjustment to us. But when we got her her forehead was all scabbed from banging her head against the wall. So she didn't start this when she came to us. Our doctor told us this child had not been fed right. She was so anemic it was no wonder she was sick all the time. So these weren't adjustment problems—there were no adjustment problems to our family. But she was not a normal child for her age. It took us six months to work her into a responsive sort of child. She couldn't figure out how to get a Cheerio from her high chair tray to her mouth. She would just sit and cry and want me to put it into her mouth. I talked to a pediatrician about this and he said it was typical of a foster child who was spoon-fed because the foster mother didn't want the child to make a mess. And you don't give the child a bunch of Cheerios because they would fall on the floor and get stepped on. So P seemed to have been bottle-fed, not given the right kind of food, and she must have been locked up in a crib or playpen because she was not mobile. Not like a normal one-year-old who zips around the house. Things began improving after about six months. But it was awfully difficult to understand her. We would play with her and tickle the bottom of her foot or put our mouth on her tummy and blow and whatever we did she would be frightened. She just couldn't understand why somebody would do something like this to her. J [older sister] was the one who pulled her out of it. Not [father] or me, but J. J is five years older than P. J and P slept in the same room, and J pulled P's crib next to hers. I'd get up in the morning and P would be in J's bed, and they'd be hugging each other. She was right there, tenderly pulling P out. And P began crawling within a week and a half, and she was up walking within two and one-half weeks. She went from just sitting. We had to teach her how to crawl at the age of one.

□ ■ □ ■

L did nothing but sit and shake. He couldn't eat with a spoon. He had nightmares for many weeks. He needs lots of care and babying.

□ ■ □ ■

One family was critical of their child's prior foster placement, but not on grounds of neglect or indifference, indeed, quite the opposite. The parents explained that S (their adopted son, who was the fifth child in the family but the only one who had been adopted) was raised with a woman who felt that, although her own son was six weeks younger, since S did not have a mother, all the attention should go to him.

So when he came, I was thinking, and I think we all felt, that to make him secure we would hold him and give him his bottles in the middle of the night. There was also this whole list of things that she [the foster mother] had sent: "He will not eat this," "He will not take medicine." So we were trying to make his adjustment easier. Instead, what we had was a child who had been overly cared for, had had so much attention. In fact, the night before he came he'd been rocked for two and a half hours. We just reinforced all of that for several months afterwards. Everybody who came in sat and held him for an hour. So we just fed it, more and more and more. The foster mother was killed three or four months later and a friend of hers who was a mutual friend of ours relayed this information to us which we didn't know and possibly the caseworker wasn't familiar with it. It concerned the friend enough, that she thought she had to tell us, what had been going on, because she realized that the child was placed with us, and that she thought it was important for us to know—and I think it was.

About half of the parents perceived problems or difficulties involving their adopted child and his or her siblings, but the large majority attributed those difficulties solely to normal sibling rivalry. The proportion did not vary with the race of the adopted child. Only 11 and 15 percent of the parents who adopted black and Indian or Asian children, respectively, attributed difficulties involving the adopted child and his or her siblings to race. The others did not perceive any problems.

For example, one family who had had a son born to them and then had adopted an older boy described the following first encounter:

The two boys were extremely close, they couldn't be closer if they were natural brothers. They fight and they bicker, and B picks on N, but at the same time is very protective of him. There has never been a problem as far as adoption. In fact, they accepted each other faster than B accepted me. He accepted N upon their first meeting and N did the same. N was sixteen months old and was in the stage when he just didn't want to go to strangers for any reason at all. B sat down in front of the television and N climbed up into his lap and it's been that way ever since. N had never seen him before in his life. He just said, "You're my brother," and climbed up into his lap and that settled it.

Another family that had two children and adopted their third told us: "They [the two children born to the parents] were very anxious to have her [the expected adopted child]. They called the social worker the "new baby lady." Everytime she would come they would run up to her and yell, "Have you got her, have you got her?" So they were very ready. I think this is partly because of our attitude. She was not an intruder, but somebody you were waiting for."

Many of the parents that adopted after they had had children used the phrase "adoption is a family affair." They meant by this that their children were participants in their discussions and in their decision to adopt, especially when the discussion focused on the age, sex, and race of the child.

When asked if their own relations to the children who were born to them had undergone any strain as a result of the adoption, more than 75 percent felt that it had not. Again, the race of the child adopted did not differentiate parents' responses to this question.

Friends and neighbors were perceived by the parents as having little interest in or reaction to their adopted child. Only about 10 percent of the parents reported that they had received negative feedback from either neighbors or friends as a result of their decision to adopt transracially. Forty-seven percent of the parents reported that they had had social contacts with families who had adopted transracially before they adopted their first nonwhite child. For most of the families, the contact was a casual friendship or a professional relationship. One couple reported that their adoption of a black child cost them the friendship of a couple they had considered their best friends.

Another family reported that after they brought their black child home they received an ultimatum from the City Council ordering them to leave town. The family called the FBI for protection. They continued to live where they had been and, although their relations with neighbors and others is not friendly, they and their children have not been victims of insults or violence. And another family who described their neighborhood as "exclusive" was surprised that they had *not* received any hate mail or obscene phone calls or found insults scrawled on their house.

The reactions of relatives, however, and the parents' responses to these reactions, were more complicated. Twenty-eight percent of the parents perceived grandparents and aunts and uncles as approving and positive about their decision from the outset. Thirty-five percent said that most of their close relatives assumed an initially negative and disapproving stance, but were coming around to the point where they acknowledged their own relationship to the adopted child; and the families were on speaking, and generally friendly, terms. Both of these groups probably include relatives who were just mystified or surprised by their children's or nieces' or nephews' behavior. This was especially the case in families in which the couple had borne children.

Of the remaining 37 percent, 31 percent said that their close relatives still rejected the adopted child and were not reconciled with the parents. The other 6 percent reported that contacts had been resumed, but the parents felt that the relations were nervous and apprehensive in their interaction with the child and with them. One set of parents who were still not reconciled with their children's grandparent related an incident in which the father's father had telephoned the adoption agency just prior to the time a black child was to be placed in his son's home and informed them that he "did not want them placing a nigger child in his family."

Another mother explained that each of the three times they announced their plans to adopt a nonwhite child her parents were "shocked"; the shock lasted for approximately three weeks. And another told us that her mother believed "she was doing this [adopting a black child, when she could bear her own children] to hurt her."

Some parents described comical instances in which the grandparents were at first shocked, hostile, rejecting, and so on, and then came to love and feel attached to their new grandchild. Their general attitude, however, as expressed in the language they used when talking about blacks or Indians or Asians did not alter at all. They still referred to blacks as "niggers" and to Asians as "gooks" or "chinks," and they still continued to make derogatory remarks about the laziness, dumbness, untrustworthiness, and so on of such people.

Respondents who had become reconciled with their parents after a period of estrangement described elaborate arrangement they had worked out whereby they did not visit their parents at their parents' home (usually when it was in another city) or, if they visited them, they did not sleep in their parents' house.

None of the respondents reported accepting a compromise which would have involved the grandparents relating to the natural grandchildren but not to the adopted grandchildren. And none of the parents indicated that they had included their parents in the decision-making process. In other words, none of them told us that, when initially considering the idea of adopting a nonwhite child, or indeed when they had pretty much made up their minds to try to adopt such a child, they had consulted with their parents or asked them for an opinion or advice. In almost all instances the grandparents were informed of the parents' decision after the adoption agency had told them a specific child was available and it was only a matter of weeks (or even less) before the child would be placed in their home.

The parents were also asked if they had perceived any change in their own self-image, in their attitudes and beliefs, and in their friends since the adoption. Sixty-three percent claimed that some changes had occurred in their personality and in their attitudes; an additional 19 percent recognized some changes in themselves but attributed it to the fact that they had become parents for the first time. Most of the 63 percent who attributed the changes in themselves to the fact that they had adopted transracially claimed that they had become more racially and socially sensitive. They felt that they had become more aware of manifestations of prejudice, and they believed more strongly than they did before in the importance of treating people alike and not emphasizing distinctions that stemmed from racial characteristics.

A few parents said the adoption had made them realize how prejudiced they had been and to some extent still were. The difference was now that they were parents of a black child they felt they must face up to their prejudice and in most instances do something about it. One family put it this way, "We have to work extra hard to stomp out this residue of racial bigotry in ourselves."

Another family, however, insisted, "We just don't identify with the black community. We don't care much about racial attitudes. We know we will not be accepted by the black community. I guess the big change is that we are much more aware of our feelings and we do try less often to think of ourselves as white."

Most of the families talked about how adopting a black or Indian child had made them "color blind," meaning that they no longer noticed or tended to separate people by color.

Whatever changes the parents reported in themselves for the most part did not result in institutional changes. Respondents did not claim that they had joined new organizations or stopped attending those to which they had belonged. The main organizational or institutional change that occurred in their lives was that they had joined the Open Door Society. A few families mentioned that they had established closer ties to their church or that they had joined another church, one in which they felt their adopted child would be more readily accepted.

The family that adopted the child suffering from PKU reported that their church is and had been a major source of support for them: "They [the congregation] have gone out of their way to keep C in the Sunday School and she feels very much at home there."

A common reason given by couples who say they want to adopt a child but will accept only a white child is that nonwhites have a harder time in American society. Thus, although they feel that they would be able to offer a nonwhite child a good home and emotional security while he or she is still young, they are convinced that they could not protect the child from the barbs and taunts that would be directed at him or her during adolescence and adulthood. Such couples might also argue that a nonwhite child who has grown up in a middle-class, white environment is less capable of coping with problems involving race than one who has grown up "with his or her own people" and experienced rejection and discrimination more gradually from childhood onward. This of course is an argument often cited by blacks who oppose transracial adoption. We thought it would be especially interesting therefore to find out how many parents who had made a decision contrary to this line of reasoning perceived their adopted child's future.

We asked first about problems the parents foresee or anticipate when their child reaches adolescence. Seventy percent said that they had given this question considerable thought before adopting and had decided to adopt even though they recognized that their family and their child would be confronted with serious problems. About 12 percent expressed the hope that American society would change significantly so that the prejudice and discrimination that they recognize exists today would be diminished to the extent that their child would not suffer from it. To support this hope, they pointed to the changes that had occurred institutionally in the United States (largely as a result of the Supreme Court decision in Brown vs. Board of Education) and in the informed attitudes and feelings that they had seen manifested since the end of World War II. One family said simply, "We're betting on a good world."

But the great majority expected that their adopted child would experience rejection by many groups that comprise white society and that rejection would be especially strong on the part of the parents of their white friends. They also expected that adolescence would be the first time their child would undergo a crisis about his or her identity. Overwhelmingly, however, the parents believe that the type of home life they provide for the children before they reach adolescence, and the emotional security with which they endow them, will see them through the crisis.

The following observation was made by parents who had adopted a black boy.

He'll have a lot of problems. First, he'll have the normal problems, which are tremendous of course; and then added to that he'll have the racial problems out here in a white community especially. There are some people who don't favor social integration on a one-to-one basis. These people are afraid of their daughters being impregnated by black males. They are afraid of a black touching them. There are all kinds of weird fears. He'll have conflicts with bigoted teachers. There are Archie Bunkers in the school system and in the teaching profession, just as there are in all professions. Maybe moreso in our community because it's 98 percent white. They are not made aware of their own deficiencies. So they go on reinforcing them year after year and maybe go through their entire lifetimes without realizing they're an Archie Bunker. But when D comes along he's going to make them aware of that. I presume we'll have problems with sex and problems with teaching, and problems with certain homes where he wants to go; those will all be negative aspects.

Most of the parents believed that by the time their adopted children become adults they will have worked out their relations with the larger society such that they will feel secure and well adjusted. Twenty-five percent believed that their children will be able to marry anyone they choose, and that color will not present exclusive barriers. The others would not commit themselves and claimed only that their child would find his or her place and would make a workable adjustment. How many of these statements were wishful thinking on the parents' part, and how many of them were deliberate convictions, was hard to determine.[13]

For whatever weight one may wish to attach to it, it is worth commenting on the fact that the parents in the Grow and Shapiro survey also conveyed this sense of optimism about the future in general and about the ability and motivation of their adopted children to adjust to the complex status their color and adoption have imposed on them.

The last topic focused directly on the issue of racial identity: that of the adopted child, the parents, and the family. We asked the parents with which racial category, if any, their adopted child identified. Did he think of himself as black, as Indian, as Korean, and so on?

Seventy-nine percent of the parents who had adopted a white child said that the child considered himself white. Thirty-two percent of the parents who adopted a black child said that the child considered himself black, and 36 percent of the parents who adopted an Indian, an Asian, or a child from some other racial category said that the child identified with that category. The parents' responses to questions concerning their perception of their adopted child's racial identity are shown in Table 4.9.

Even though objectively there is no difference in the age ranges of the white and nonwhite children, Table 4.9 shows that 38 and 30 percent of the parents of nonwhite children claimed that their child was too young to have acquired a racial identity, compared to 7 percent of the parents of a white child. We interpreted this as meaning that parents who had adopted black, Indian, and Asian children were less sure of their child's racial identity than parents of white children.

The parents' responses to the question, "With which race would you like to see your adopted child identify?" may also be interpreted as being ambivalent, because 11 percent of the parents who were talking about a white child said that they had no preference, compared to 24 percent who were describing a black child and 34 percent who were describing an Indian or Asian child. Thirty-one and 35 percent of the parents who were describing black or Indian or Asian children said that they wanted them to identify as blacks or American Indians or Koreans; the others had no preference, or wanted them to identify with their own race and with the race of their adopted family, or with the human race.

It appears then that, save for approximately one-third who said specifically that they wanted their child to identify with the race that matched the child's physical characteristics, the preferences of the other parents had little likelihood of being fulfilled. It is not realistic for a black child in the United States to have two racial identities, and identifying with the human race has

TABLE 4.9 Parents' perceptions of first adopted child's racial identity, by the race of the child

Parents' Responses	White	Black	American Indian-Asian, Other
	(In Percent)		
Too young	7	38	30
Confused	11	11	11
White	75	5	11
Black	--	32	8
American-Indian	--	--	15
Asian	--	--	7
Mexican, Puerto Rican,	--	--	14
Don't know	4	8	7
Total	100	100	100

not proven to be a useful substitute thus far in American society which still places important distinctions on racial characteristics.

The family quoted earlier who said that there was no way they could raise their child as a black man talked about their son's identity in the following manner.

That's the problem I was talking about before. I guess its not so much what we would like. It's that we just don't identify with the black community. We're not against the black community, its just we don't have the background. We don't think we'll be able to instill in D the identity of the black community—we're not going to raise him deliberately as a white person, but I'm sure he will be one just because we are. What I hope is that when he decides to try out his blackness, and I'm sure he will—to see how he is accepted by the black community—I hope we will be in a close enough relationship that I can learn from him.

More typical responses about their child's racial identity as an adult are the following:

It's his decision, not ours. Hopefully, we will raise him with an identity toward both groups because he is both white and Negro and if he wants to identify with one group that's his decision. I would hope that as a mulatto child, and since there are many mulatto children, that he might feel a part of a new kind of race, and of having the potential of both races within him, such as exists in Hawaii where the people are all mixed races. I would feel better if he chose to identify with the blacks than if he chose to identify with the whites, because I really feel that if he tries to pass for white we have not done our jobs as parents. But if he wants to identify with blacks this is legitimate because legally he is a Negro child and as far as society now exists in 1972 he is a Negro child. To most whites, he is not a mixed race. So therefore, I can't say what society will be like in twenty years from now, but as it is right now, hopefully he will identify with the Negro race simply because that's what he is now. Society views him as Negro.

□ ■ □ ■

I think he should identify with Indians. He is Indian. There's no reason why he shouldn't. I don't feel that identifying with one means he has to reject the other, however, I think it will depend a lot upon where he's living. If there are other Indians around he'll probably identify with them. I think too—he'll probably have fairly close contact with both. I don't think he can avoid that his family is white, and most of the people in town are white. I would guess that if there is an Indian group that he will be a member of it. And after that I have no idea, how close. . . .

□ ■ □ ■

He's Indian, hopefully he'll feel proud of being an Indian and be interested in being with other Indians. Maybe somewhat resentful that he didn't grow up with other Indians, and therefore seek them out. I don't think there's any guessing as to how big a thing it will be in his mind. It will probably depend a lot upon what happens in the next ten or fifteen years—in terms of general society as much as anything else.

Another family who adopted an American Indian commented that they really did not see much likelihood of their child identifying with the Indian culture because there is no contemporary American Indian culture and it would be foolish and harmful to identify with the white community's definition of this culture.

But 75 percent of the parents claimed that they were doing various things in order to have their adopted child learn about and identify with the race into which he or she was born. The most common efforts involved bringing books, pictures, toys, and music into their homes, along with cultural artifacts associated with or helpful in describing the child's race. In addition, they have joined the Open Door Society and they make arrangements for their child to play with other nonwhite children on a regular basis. Since such children are not usually available in their immediate neighborhood, this typically involves contacting Open Door Society families and then transporting children by car.

The following responses on the part of a family who had adopted an American Indian child represent an elaborately worked out program:

We're reading a lot of books. We are also buying books so he will have easy access to them once he gets older. We just got some small pamphlets put out by the Vermillion Indians in South Dakota which have concepts of Indian culture in them. Probably on the 4-, 5-, 6-year old level. We've had some contact with the Indian community. We talked to a girl who called about COAC stuff and we said we were interested. We arranged a picnic for Indian families and families that had adopted Indian kids. When the Sioux kids who were going around through the Youth Understanding Exchange were in town we went over to see their show and talked with them. It's mostly a matter of trying to explain Indianess to him and letting him meet other Indians so he can see they are real people. We try to avoid TV shows that have Indians on them, unless there is a very unusual one and it has an historically correct view. It's hard at his age level. It goes through and gets lost. We went to the Pow Wow last summer and the ones who were dressed up were fine, but the others he didn't think were Indians. I think we're doing O.K. so far. A year ago I would have said no. But I think its come this year.

The family with the PKU-affected Indian child described their efforts:

I guess we don't care. I don't think we are really hung up on the racial thing. We'd like for C to identify herself as a person. She's very pretty and it's too bad she feels so angry. Whether we can be so liberal if it comes to the point of her marrying a black man, I don't know.

We did try to get some information about Indians. We talk about Indian arts and crafts; we had a black friend who we helped through school. She did babysitting for us. We kept contact with her; we have been fairly close. We try to spot black neighbors and we do keep up with COAC picnics where there are interracial families. We try to keep in contact with people who have mixed racial children. (Father) Where I work we have a few blacks, not many. We have international friends, we have Pakistani friends, Indian friends, from Jamaica.

I think as long as C is so angry it's difficult to know. We would hope and pray that through the years that other friends would help her. We had all these naive notions that by being positive about adoption, positive about people with other racial backgrounds and friends and children, that would help. We have bought some storybooks and tried to have things available to show blacks and white. She very definitely thinks of herself as a black child in a white family and we might as well face it and accept it.

About 12 percent of the parents self-consciously and openly stated that they are living and plan to continue to live as they would have if they had not adopted a child of a different race. They do not bring artifacts into their homes that are representative of other cultures or ways of life, and they do not seek out black children for the purpose of providing special friendships for their nonwhite child. Their main objective is to bring the child into their life-style—to have him or her become a full-fledged member of the family. Thus far, they have not changed, nor do they have any plans to change, their own life-style. The parents who assumed this position are as likely to have adopted a black child as an American Indian or Korean child. There was no homogeneity of response on the basis of the race of the adopted child.

We noted earlier that 32 percent of the parents who had adopted a black child perceived the child as identifying as a black person, and 44 percent of the parents who had adopted an Indian or Asian child perceived the child as identifying with the race into which he or she was born. A smaller percentage of both of these groups expected these identities to continue into adulthood as witnessed by their responses to the question, "What is your guess about the future; when your child is an adult with which racial group do you think he or she will identify?" Twenty-six percent of the parents who had adopted a black child said black, and 22 percent of the parents who had adopted an Asian or Indian child thought their child would retain that identity as an adult. Not all the remaining parents thought their child would become a "white adult"; indeed, only about 35 percent in both groups said they thought he or she would become "white." The remaining 40 percent or so felt that the child was too young for them to look that far ahead into the future, or said that they were hopeful that the child would identify with both black and white, or Indian and white, or Korean and white. On further probing it turned out that practically all the parents who expected their adopted child to identify with the race into which he or she was born also believed that the child's physical characteristics, skin pigment, hair, eyes, nose, and so on, would make it impossible for him or her to become "white."

In the final series of questions, the emphasis shifted from the child's identity to that of the parents and of the family. About themselves the parents were asked, "Did your racial identity change after you adopted [name of child]?'' Seventy percent said that it did not—that they still consider themselves white. About 30 percent said that the adoption had the effect of making them lose their sense of identity with any objective racial category, and that they now identified only with the human race. In about 5 percent of the families, the identity of one parent shifted to the race of the adopted child and that of the other remained unchanged.

The same question was asked about the identity of the family. Sixty-nine of the parents said that their family's racial identity had changed as a result of the adoption. The most common response was that the family perceived its racial identity as ''mixed''; 44 percent responded in this way. Twenty-two percent said that the family now identified with the human race and that it had no racial identity in the manner in which the term is typically applied.[14] The race of the child they adopted was not related to the parents' responses.

The couple who had spent some time in Africa in the Peace Corps had thought about their white identity quite a lot and were uncomfortable with it. The mother said:

I became concerned I think, with being a ''Wasp'' when I was in Africa because I saw the great discrepancies there between people. I felt I was in the minority and I felt a hatred towards whites, particularly Americans. America is not well loved abroad. So I think I was more aware when I was in Africa, than I am now.

The last formal question that we put to the parents was intended as a ''catch all.'' It asked:

If a family like your own, in terms of religion, income, and education living in the community asked you to advise them about whether they ought to adopt a non-white child, what would your advice be?

Save for 7 percent who answered that as a matter of principle they would not advise anyone on such an important personal decision, all but 3 percent said they would urge the family to go ahead and adopt. The 90 percent in our survey is almost identical to the percentage (91 percent) of respondents in the Grow and Shapiro survey who also said they would urge both white and black parents to adopt transracially.

Forty percent warned that the family should be very clear in their own minds that they are not making their decision because of their belief in ''some social cause,'' ''civil rights,'' ''racial equality,'' or what have you. The parents' decision must be made on the basis of how much they wanted a child and because they believed they could offer the child a good home.

Slogans, causes, and political ideology should have no place in their decision. Most of the parents mentioned bad motives such as "proving you are liberal," "wanting to do something noble," "taking a stand against the population explosion." The good motives were the "selfish ones, including wanting a child very badly."

Some of the parents' were quite eloquent in describing what they meant.

A couple should take a child because the child needs a home and because they are selfish enough to want that child. Many of the people I've talked to have this noble ambition that they are finally doing something great for the world. But if you don't want this child very, very selfishly, as much as you want a natural child, you cannot raise him properly. At least I don't feel you can. You've got to want your adopted child every bit as much, if not more, than your natural child. And its got to be a very selfish desire—not something you're doing for the world. Because when you get down to the nitty-gritty problems of living every day, suddenly you're not thinking about the world, you're thinking about you and the child and your relationship.

The first thing I would tell them is to look into it; contact an agency first of all. The second thing is to sit down and talk for a while and just throw out questions. How are your parents going to accept this child? How do you feel about a non-white child? What facilities do you have in your home for a non-white child? How conscious are you of race and the racial problems? Questions like that do really get them thinking. Lastly, I think I'd tell them of the joys, because I think that any parent who goes into a non-white adoption should be aware of all of the problems first. Because it is not the easiest way to have children. I feel that parents should be fully aware of the problems they will face, for example, how does a parent feel when someone slights their child? Do they take it personally? Like I look on a person who says something with pity, I don't take it personally. But I think this is something parents have to think about and look through.

Even the family with the disturbed child maintained that they still believed in adoption, but that they would urge a couple to obtain as much information about the child, adopt as young a child as possible, and be sure of their own self-image.

Only one family said flatly, "We would not help any white family adopt a black child. We feel now that if a black child can find a black home that is ideal. If it were us today, knowing what we know, we would not do it."

NOTES

1. Lucille J. Grow and Deborah Shapiro, *Black Children, White Parents: A Study of Transracial Adoption*, Child Welfare League of America, New York, 1974.
2. The median age in the Grow and Shapiro survey was 34 to 37 years.

3. In the Grow and Shapiro survey, 30 percent of the parents had not had children born to them. The distribution of children in the Grow and Shapiro survey was similar to the distribution shown above.
4. Of the 56 percent who adopted more than one child, 76 percent adopted two children.
5. Public agencies under the authority of the state in which the parent lived were the source of 70 percent of first adopted children and 84 percent of second adopted children. Fifty percent of the parents received their first child through a private church agency.
6. Grow and Shapiro reported that they had found a relationship between the child's racial comfort and his appearance. The more the child looked black, the more the parents felt that the child was racially uncomfortable. Perhaps the parents' perceptions should be viewed as projections of their own discomfort.
7. The median age of the children at the time of adoption in the Grow and Shapiro survey was 13.9 months.
8. Sixty-nine percent of the parents who could not bear children adopted more than one child; 48 percent adopted at least three children.
9. An illustration of this is the family who felt they had been pressured into adopting a black child because they were told that black families were much less likely to adopt children than white families.
10. In fact, 69 percent obtained children who were less than one year old.
11. Grow and Shapiro, op. cit., footnote 1, p. 87.
12. PKU is a rare human genetic disease marked by the inability to oxidize phenylpyruvic acid and by severe mental deficiency.
13. One family felt that if their son tried to become part of the black community he would not be accepted. They said, "There's no way we can raise him as a black man."
14. Three percent said their family identified as black.

CHAPTER FIVE

STUDIES OF RACIAL IDENTITY AND ATTITUDES OF CHILDREN

This chapter presents the major issues and the important research findings concerning young children's racial preferences and identity in the United States. It is not an exhaustive review of every study that has been conducted on this topic, and it does not even attempt to present the specific findings of all the studies it mentions. It should, however, provide an appropriate framework for assessing what the state of knowledge is at the present time and what changes have occurred between 1939, when the first studies were reported, and 1975, the time of writing. It also provides comparisons, where appropriate, between studies conducted on white children reared in white homes, black children reared in black homes, and the special characteristics of the children involved in the study reported in this volume. But it is important to stress again that the child respondents described in this study are different from any of those with which they are compared because all of them have parents and siblings of a race different from their own. Comparisons for this reason may be especially useful.

Empirical studies of young children's racial attitudes and identity extend almost five decades. Judith Porter states that Bruno Lasker in 1929 was the first "serious investigator" to study the racial awareness of preschool children.[1] But Porter claims that Lasker's conclusion that "children up to the age of eight are ignorant of racial differences" is questionable, because "he studies not the children themselves but adults' reminiscences of childhood experiences and teachers' observations of elementary school subjects."[2]

A decade after Lasker's study, Ruth Horowitz studied a sample of nursery school children and found that they had a sense of social awareness. Her observations, however, were based on 24 subjects.[3]

The work of Kenneth and Mamie Clark, which began in the late 1930s, involved the use of white and brown dolls to study the racial preferences, awareness, and identity of white and black children.[4] Their early work serves as a benchmark for most of the subsequent studies of young children's attitudes and awareness. The basic design the Clarks employed involved presenting black subjects between the ages of about three and seven with white and brown baby dolls and asking the children to, "Give me the doll that . . ."

1. You like to play with best
2. Is a nice doll
3. Looks bad
4. Is a nice color
5. Looks like a colored child
6. Looks like a Negro child
7. Looks like a white child
8. Looks like you

Items 1 through 4 were intended to measure racial attitudes; items 5 through 7, racial awareness; and item 8, racial identity. With variations, such as the introduction of a third doll with skin lighter than that of the brown doll, or the use of dolls other than baby dolls, this technique for measuring young children's attitudes and awareness about race has been used up to the present time by researchers in the United States, New Zealand, South Africa, and England.

The Clarks' basic results are shown in Table 5.1.

TABLE 5.1 Percentage of children selecting the white doll

Request for	Percent Selecting White Doll
1. Doll most like to play with	67
2. The nice doll	59
3. The bad doll	17
4. The doll that is a nice color	60
5. The doll that looks white	94
6. The doll that looks colored	6
7. The doll that looks Negro	20
8. The doll that looks like you	33

Source: K. B. Clark and M. P. Clark "Racial Identification and Preference
in Negro Children" in Readings in Social Psychology (New York
Henry Holt and Company, 1947), p. 171, Table 1, p. 175, Table 5.

On the items that measure racial preferences or attitudes (1 through 4), most of the children exhibited a white bias. On the items that measure awareness (5 through 7), almost all the children indicated their ability to differentiate skin color. On the item that measures identification (8), two-thirds of the children identified themselves accurately.

When the children were divided into homogeneous age categories, the Clarks found that older children were more likely to identify themselves correctly and to distinguish the white doll from the brown doll. But age made little difference in the attitude items. The older children were as likely to express pro-white attitudes as were the younger ones (Table 5.2).

Skin shade, however, did differentiate responses on some of the preference items and on self-identity. As the percentages in Table 5.3 indicate, the lighter-skinned children were more likely to prefer and to identify with the white dolls than were the darker-skinned children. Responses to the awareness items revealed no differences by skin shade.

The Clarks concentrated their studies on black children, mostly in segre-

TABLE 5.2 Percentage of children selecting the white doll, by age

Request for Doll	Age of Respondent Percentage Selecting White				
	3	4	5	6	7+
Play with the best	55	76	74	71	60
Nice Doll	58	76	72	53	52
Looks Bad	19	24	11	15	17
Nice Color	58	72	78	56	48
Looks White	77	86	94	97	100
Looks Colored	13	17	7	4	0
Looks Negro	29	35	30	17	7
Looks Like You	61	31	52	32	13

Source: K. B. Clark and M. P. Clark "Racial Identification and
Preference in Negro Children" in Readings in Social Psychology
(New York: Henry Holt and Company, 1947), p. 172, Table 2;
p. 176, Table 6.

gated southern schools, more than 30 years ago. Their basic findings, however, that black children prefer white to black have been replicated in practically every study of young children's racial attitudes up to and including the present time. Only recently, in the last four or five years, has there been evidence that *older* black children, those in junior high and high school, exhibit preferences for black, and positive, self-images. Those findings are described later.

Greenwald and Oppenheim thought that part of the explanation for the high percentage of incorrect self-identification among the children in the Clarks' studies may have been the lack of an appropriate doll with which the lighter-skinned black children could identify.[5] They decided to repeat the Clarks' experiment but, instead of having only two dolls (dark brown and white), they used three dolls (dark brown, medium brown, and white). In addition, the questions the experimenters asked were more open-ended, for

TABLE 5.3 Percentage of children selecting the white doll, by skin shade

Request for Doll	Skin Shading		
	Light	Medium	Dark
Play with the best	76	67	61
Nice doll	67	56	60
Looks bad	13	17	18
Nice color	70	53	65
Looks white	94	92	96
Looks colored	9	6	4
Looks Negro	20	21	18
Looks like you	80	26	19

Source: K. B. Clark and M. P. Clark "Racial Identification and Preference

in Negro Children" in Readings in Social Psychology (New York

Henry Holt and Company, 1947), p. 173, Table 3, p. 176, Table 7.

example, "Is there a doll that . . . ," instead of, "Give me the doll that. . . ." Their subjects were 75 nursery school children between the ages of three and five. Thirty-nine were black and 36 were white. The results are reported in Table 5.4.

Greenwald and Oppenheim concluded on the basis of the responses shown that "these similarities to the previous researchers' results indicate high reliability over time. . . . Apparently then, different samples and sample size, the difference of an entire generation, the use of different dolls and also white examiners did not bring about appreciable different answers to the basic questions."[6]

But changes did occur with regard to the identification item. As the results in Table 5.5 show, only 13 percent of the black children misidentified themselves, compared to 36 percent of the Clarks' northern black sample. The use of a light-skinned black doll, then, played a role in reducing the percentage of misidentification. The authors concluded that "Negro children do not manifest an unusual tendency to misidentify themselves. How-

TABLE 5.4 Negro and white children's responses to initial questions about racial dolls

Questions	Dolls	Negro Children	White Children
		(In Percent)	
1. Doll want to play with	Dark	28	22
	Medium	13	4
	White	56	63
2. Doll do not want to play with	D	14	31
	M	56	51
	W	12	4
3. Doll that is good	D	35	20
	M	15	3
	W	50	69
4. Doll that is bad	D	21	26
	M	50	51
	W	10	3
5. Doll that is nice color	D	31	18
	M	8	8
	W	56	71
6. Doll that is not nice color	D	17	37
	M	62	57
	W	13	3
7. Doll that looks like white child	D	5	0
	M	3	17
	W	90	78
8. Doll that looks like colored child	D	73	54
	M	19	54
	W	5	6

Source: H. J. Greenwald and D. B. Oppenheim, "Reported Magnitude of Self- Misidentification among Negro Children - Artifact?" (in Journal of Personality and Social Psychology, Vol. 8, 1968), p. 50, Table 1.

ever, the similarity of the evaluative responses in all the studies corroborates the unpopularity of the Negro's skin color among children."[7]

Mary Ellen Goodman studied the racial attitudes of four-year-old black children attending nursery schools in a city in the northeastern United States. She reported in 1952:

Basically our Negro children are out-group oriented. Through all the individual variations there runs this common thread. . . . These children share a fundamental orientation—a sense of direction away from Negroes and toward Whites.

Our Whites are in-group oriented. Individual orientations among them are as great as among the Negroes but this they have in common. . . . Racially speaking they are

TABLE 5.5 Percentage of negro and white children's selections of the doll which looked like them

Doll Colors	Negro Children by Skin Color			Total Negro Children	White Children[a]
	Light	Medium	Dark		
Greenwald and Oppenheim					
Dark Brown	22	50	43	41	19
Mulatto	56	19	50	38	25
White	11	25	0	13	47
(N)	(9)	(16)	(14)	(39)	(36)
Clark and Clark Study					
Dark Brown	20	73	81	63	--
White	80	26	19	36	--
(N)	(46)	(126)	(79)	(253)	--

[a]White children misidentified themselves more than Negro children in the present study (X^2=16.29, df-2, P<.0001).

Source: H. J. Greenwald and D. B. Oppenheim, "Reported Magnitude of Self-Misidentification among Negro Children - Artifact?" (in Journal of Personality and Social Psychology, Vol. 8, 1968), p. 51, Table 2.

complacent about the self. Their basic orientation—their sense of direction is around and within the orbit of the White world.[8]

Goodman concluded on this note: "It is all too clear that Negro children not yet five can sense that they are marked, and grow uneasy. They can like enormously what they see across the color line and find it hard to like what they see on their side. In this there is scant comfort or security; and in it are the dynamics for rending personality asunder."[9]

Twenty years later, in 1972, J. Kenneth Morland, who had been studying young children's racial attitudes for about a decade, reported the results of his study in Lynchburg, Virginia.[10] The major purpose of the 1972 study was to determine children's racial attitudes as racial balance was being instituted throughout the Lynchburg public school system. The study involved 116 children (aged three, four, and five) in nursery schools and 103 children in kindergarten and primary grades (first through third), who were interviewed by means of a series of pictures.

Racially the children were divided as follows: nursery school level, 58 white and 58 black; kindergarten and primary grades, 53 white and 50 black. The nursery school children were interviewed in school, and the kindergarten and primary grade children at home. White interviewers interviewed white children, and black interviewers interviewed black children.

The children were shown six pictures which had the following characteristics:

Picture 1. Six white children, three boys and three girls, sitting around a table eating cookies and drinking punch

Picture 2. Same as picture 1, but the children are black

Picture 3. Six men, three black and three white, in a group holding paper cups

Picture 4. Same as picture 3, but the people are women

Picture 5. Six girls, three black and three white

Picture 6. Same as picture 5, but the children are boys

Morland asked the children essentially the same questions about the pictures that the Clarks had asked their subjects about the dolls and added the following, "Which *man* looks most like your father?" and "Which *woman* looks most like your mother?"

Morland reported that the major findings of his study were: (a) Black children do not show as favorable an attitude toward their own race as white children show toward theirs. (b) Blacks are more likely to accept whites than whites are to accept blacks. (c) Compared to whites, blacks are less likely to prefer their own race, to say they would rather be children of their own race, to identify their mothers and fathers with members of their own race, and to say that children of their own race are prettier, better students, and nicer than whites. (d) On only one measure, self-identity (i.e., which child the respondents said they looked most like), did black children show no significant difference from white children. (e) Preschool blacks were less likely than in-school blacks to accept members of their own race, to prefer members of their own race, to say that they looked like members of their own race, and to say that they would rather be members of their own race. In-school and preschool children did not differ significantly on any of those measures. The data supporting these conclusions are presented in Tables 5.16 through 5.25 which appear at the end of this chapter.

In concluding his report, Morland commented:

A major finding of this study of racial attitudes among Lynchburg school children is support for the existence of an American norm that each racial-ethnic grouping of Americans should have a favorable view of itself. The movement toward this assumed norm was seen in a clear-cut way among the black American children studied. Pre-school black respondents *preferred, identified with* and had a strong bias for whites. However such preference identification and bias were significantly less among blacks in kindergarten and primary grades, and by the end of high school black Americans showed a highly favorable evaluation of and no social distance from "Black American." [11]

A few years earlier, in 1969, Morland had applied essentially the same approach to a study of racial awareness among Hong Kong Chinese children. [12] He compared the responses of the Chinese children to those made by white and black children in Connecticut and Virginia. The children ranged in age from four to six. Table 5.6 compares the responses of American Caucasian, American black, and Hong Kong Chinese children to the question, "Would you rather play with these children or with those?"

The responses indicate that all three groups differed from each other, but that a majority of the whites and Chinese preferred their own race, while a majority of the blacks preferred the other race.

When the children were asked, "Which child do you look most like?" and "Which child would you rather be?" the three groups differed significantly from each other. Both times, however, the white children were the most likely to select the child of their own race (Table 5.7).

Morland concluded:

The findings show that Hong Kong Chinese children differed significantly from both the American Caucasian and American Negro children on racial preference and on two measures of self-identification. The Hong Kong children, unlike the American Negro children, preferred and identified with members of their own race. In this way they were like the American Caucasian children, who also preferred and identified with their own race. However, the extent of such preference and identification among the Hong Kong children was significantly lower than among the American Caucasians. This pattern of response of the Hong Kong children in preferring and identifying with their own race in a less extensive way than American Caucasian subjects but in a more accepting way than American Negro subjects could be

TABLE 5.6 Racial preference of American Caucasian, American Negro, and Hong Kong Chinese children

Racial Groups	Prefer Own Race	Prefer Other Race	Preference Not Clear
	(In Percent)		
American Caucasian[a]	82.0	12.0	6.0
American Negro	28.0	53.3	18.7
Hong Kong Chinese[b]	65.3	25.3	9.3

[a]Significant difference from each of other two groupings at the .001 level by the x^2 test.

[b]American children chose between Caucasian and Negro; Hong Kong children chose between Caucasian and Chinese.

Source: J. Kenneth Morland, "Race Awareness among American and Hong Kong Chinese Children" (American Journal of Sociology, Vol. 75, No. 3, Nov., 1969), p. 365, Table 3.

logically expected in a society with races in parallel positions. In such a society there is no dominant race to maintain its superior position and no subordinate race to show unconscious preference for and identification with the dominant race.[13]

In *Black Child-White Child*, Judith Porter's 1974 study of preschool children's racial attitudes and identities, the subjects were 175 white and 184 black children who attended 16 kindergarten and nursery schools in the Boston area. They came from middle, working, and lower-class (Aid to Dependent Children) families. Porter concluded that "even before they [preschool children] have a sophisticated knowledge of racial categories, children of both races have a positive evaluation of 'white' and a negative feeling about 'brown.' Color associations and their cultural connotations are important influences on these preferences."[14]

A major intervening variable introduced in Porter's study was social class.

TABLE 5.7   Percentage of children answering own race

Racial Group	Item A -- Look Like	Item B -- Rather be
American white	77 (In Percent)	77
American black	47	33
Hong Kong Chinese	36	54

Source: J. Kenneth Morland, "Race Awareness among American and Hong Kong

Chinese Children" (American Journal of Sociology, Vol. 75,

No. 3, Nov., 1969), pp. 366-67, Tables 4 and 5.

In addition to race, age, and sex, she wanted to know how socioeconomic status affected racial attitudes and identity. In the analysis of variance in Table 5.8, preferences are reported on the basis of responses to the doll selection items by the race, age, sex, and social class of the respondent. Porter's findings show that more white children in each sex, age, and class category preferred dolls of their own race than did black children.

Controlling for the effects of various segregated and integrated environments, Porter found that light-skinned children exhibited more own-race preferences in segregated settings than did dark-skinned children but, in desegregated settings, light-skinned children exhibited fewer own-race preferences than did dark-skinned children (Table 5.9).

Porter further hypothesized that more black than white children would reject themselves on a racial basis, that more black children would be ambivalent toward their minority group status, and that more black children would exhibit incorrect self-identification than would their white peers. As the analysis of variance in Table 5.10 indicates, these hypotheses were supported. After controlling for sex, class, and age, there was a difference by race in correctness of self-classification which was significant at the .01 level.

In 1967, Williams and Roberson reported the results of their study of 111 white children aged three through seven who responded to 24 sets of pictures.[15] Each set contained two pictures of the same object, but colored differently. In half of the sets one of the objects was white and the other black. The other 12 sets were dummies and were colored red, green, blue,

TABLE 5.8 Attitudes toward own race: controlling for sex, social class, race, and age

Race of Respondents[a]	Males								
	Middle Class			Working Class			Lower Class		
	3 yrs	4 yrs	5 yrs	3 yrs	4 yrs	5 yrs	3 yrs	4 yrs	5 yrs
White	1.39[b]	1.29	1.31	1.50	1.31	1.24	1.39	1.33	1.26
	N=3	N=14	N=23	N=1	N=8	N=12	N=3	N=4	N=11
Negro	1.72	1.67	1.82	1.53	1.56	1.51	1.83	1.63	1.67
	N=3	N=7	N=10	N=5	N=17	N=15	N=1	N=12	N=5
	Females								
White	1.46	1.27	1.28	1.33	1.19	1.19	1.17	1.31	1.25
	N=8	N=21	N-20	N=3	N=11	N=9	N=1	N=12	N=10
Negro	1.58	1.69	1.58	1.53	1.58	1.71	1.44	1.63	1.81
	N=4	N=18	N=4	N=11	N=24	N=7	N=7	N=14	N=6

[a]Total race effect, controlling for age, sex, and class:
White = 1.30, Negro = 1.64, p < .01.

[b]1 = High own-race preference; 2 = Low own-race preference.

Source: Judith D. R. Porter, Black Child, White Child: The Development of Racial Attitudes (Harvard University Press, 1971), pp. 64-65, Table 5

orange, and so on. A two-line story was attached to each set of pictures, and each story ended with the experimenter asking the child to choose the object that was *bad, dirty,* or *pretty.* The adjectives were adopted from the evaluative scales developed by Charles Osgood et al.[16] The children's scores as reported by the Williams-Roberson study are shown in Table 5.11.

Note that 75 percent of the children consistently attributed a positive adjective (pretty, nice, good) to the white pictures and a negative adjective (bad, mean, ugly) to the black pictures. According to the authors, age did not significantly affect the children's responses.

Hraba and Grant, in 1970, reproduced the Clark and Clark doll-selection study, using as their subjects black and white nursery school and kindergar-

TABLE 5.9 Attitudes toward own race: controlling for color, class, and social contact

| Setting | Light-Skinned | | |
	Middle	Working	Lower
Segregated	1.65	1.53	1.61
	N=11	N=5	N=10
Desegregated	1.77	1.61	1.73
	N=11	N=18	N=3
	Dark-Skinned		
Segregated	1.76	1.58	1.68
	N=17	N=26	N=17
Desegregated	1.50	1.52	1.55 .
	N=6	N=30	N=13

1=High own-race preference, 2=Low own-race preference

Source: Judith D. R. Porter, Black Child, White Child: The Development of Racial Attitudes (Harvard University Press, 1971), p. 102, Table 15.

ten children in Lincoln, Nebraska.[17] Their findings showed: (a) White children were significantly more ethnocentric on items 1 and 2 ("Which doll would you most like to play with?" and "Which doll is the nice doll?"). (b) There were no significant differences between black and white children on item 3 ("Which doll looks bad?"). (c) Black children were more ethnocentric on item 4 ("Which doll is a nice color?"). (See Table 5.12).

In their conclusion these authors assert that their findings indicate that important changes are occurring among black children, and that future studies will show even more strongly that blacks are proud of their identity.

Indeed, some support for their belief may be available already as witnessed by the results reported in Rosenberg and Simmons' Black and White Self-Esteem: The Urban School Child (1971).[18] In their survey of about 1900 black and white Baltimore school children ranging from the third to the

TABLE 5.10 Self-identification: controlling for sex, class, race, and age

Race of Respondents	Males Middle Class 3 yrs	4 yrs	5 yrs	Working Class 3 yrs	4 yrs	5 yrs	Lower Class 3 yrs	4 yrs	5 yrs
White	1.67	1.43	1.57	2.0	1.50	1.42	2.0	1.50	1.63
	N=3	N=14	N=23	N=1	N=8	N=12	N=3	N=4	N=4
Negro	1.67	1.71	1.60	1.60	1.47	1.53	2.0	1.50	1.40
	N=3	N=7	N=10	N=5	N=17	N=15	N=1	N=12	N=5
	Females								
White	1.50	1.57	1.30	1.33	1.45	1.33	1.0	1.50	1.40
	N=8	N=21	N=20	N=3	N=11	N=9	N=1	N=12	N=10
Negro	2.0	1.89	1.75	1.64	1.75	1.57	1.43	1.50	2.0
	N=4	N=18	N=4	N=11	N=24	N=7	N=3	N=14	N=6

1=correct self-identification, 2=incorrect self-identification.

Source: Judith D. R. Porter, Black Child, White Child: The Development of Racial Attitudes (Harvard University Press, 1971), pp. 116–17, Table 16.

twelfth grades, they found that more black than white children enjoyed high self-esteem (Table 5.13).

Rosenberg and Simmons defined self-esteem in the following terms: "Does the respondent feel that he is a person of worth? How highly does he regard himself, not as a black or white, but in general? Does he have fundamental respect for himself, appreciating his own merit, even though he is aware of faults in himself which he hopes and expects to overcome?"[19]

Black students who attended predominantly black schools enjoyed higher self-esteem than black students in schools that were predominately white. These authors were surprised to find no relationship between the respondents' estimate of self-esteem and their perception of how most Americans rank the racial group to which they belong. In other words, respondents who believed blacks are ranked first and those who believed they are ranked last did not differ in their estimate of their own self-esteem.

TABLE 5.11 Percentage of white children who attributed positive and negative adjectives to black and white pictures

Adjectives	White Pictures	Black Pictures
	(In Percent)	
Pretty	87	13
Clean	85	15
Nice	84	16
Smart	82	18
Good	81	19
Kind	76	24
Ugly	17	83
Dirty	16	84
Naughty	18	82
Stupid	18	82
Bad	15	85
Mean	10	90

Source: J. E. Williams and J. K. Roberson, "A Method for Assessing Racial Attitudes in Preschool Children" (Education and Psychological Measurement, Vol. 27, 1967), p. 685, Table 4.

Consistent with findings reported in earlier studies, black respondents associated attractiveness with light skin. When asked, "Who in your family has the nicest skin color?" and "Is he or she lighter or darker than you?" 74 percent said that the relative with the "nicest skin color" was lighter than the respondent. Seventy percent of the respondents who were judged by the interviewers to have light skins considered themselves "very or pretty good looking," compared to 47 percent of the respondents who were judged to be dark-skinned.[20]

But, there was little relationship between the respondents' judgment of

TABLE 5.12   Hraba and Grant results (1970) compared with Clark and Clark results (1939)

Dolls	Clark and Clark (1939) Blacks	Hraba and Grant (1969) Blacks	(1939-1969) x^2 Blacks	Hraba and Grant (1969) Whites
(Play with)				
1. White doll	67 (169)	30 (27)	36.2 p <.001	83 (59)
Black doll	32 (83)	70 (62)		16 (11)
(Nice doll)				
2. White doll	59 (150)	46 (41)	5.7 p <.02	70 (50)
Black doll	38 (97)	54 (48)		30 (21)
(Looks bad)				
3. White doll	17 (42)	61 (54)	43.5 p <.001	34 (24)
Black doll	59 (149)	36 (32)		63 (45)
(Nice color)				
4. White doll	60 (151)	31 (28)	23.1 p <.001	48 (34)
Black doll	38 (96)	69 (61)		49 (35)

Note: Individuals failing to make either choice not included, hence percentages
       add to less than 100.

Source: Joseph Hraba and Geoffrey Grant, "Black is Beautiful" (in
         Journal of Personality and Social Psychology, Vol. 16,
         No. 30, 1970), p. 399, Table 1.

their own skin color and their self-esteem. As the data in Table 5.14 indicate, the self-esteem of children who designated themselves "very dark" was just as high as that of the large bulk of children who said they were "a little dark" or "a little light," though lower than that of the small self-designated "very light" group.

According to Rosenberg and Simmons, the factor that had an unequivocal impact on black self-esteem was the belief a black student held about how he or she was evaluated by others such as parents, peers, and teachers. In a composite table (Table 5.15) which ranks the child's perceptions of how he or she is perceived by all these significant others, from most favorable (thinks I am wonderful) to unfavorable (thinks I am not nice), the results show that

TABLE 5.13 Self-esteem, by race

Self-Esteem	Black	White
	(In Percent)	
Low	19	37
Medium	35	30
High	40	33
	N=1,213	N=682

Source: Morris Rosenberg and Roberta G. Simmons, <u>Black and White Self-Esteem: The Urban School Child</u> (American Sociological Association, 1968), p. 5, Table 1-1.

TABLE 5.14 Child's judgment of own skin color

Self-Esteem	Very Dark	A Little Dark	A Little Light	Very Light
	(In Percent)			
Low	15	20	20	19
Medium	42	33	37	19
High	44	47	44	62
N	48	524	467	26

Source: Morris Rosenberg and Roberta G. Simmons, <u>Black and White Self-Esteem: The Urban School Child</u> (American Sociological Association, 1968), p. 52, Table 5-8.

TABLE 5.15 Self-esteem and attitudes attributed to significant others, by race

Self-Esteem	Blacks				Whites			
	Favorable		Unfavorable		Favorable		Unfavorable	
	1	2	3	4	1	2	3	4
	(In Percent)							
Low	4	13	26	38	38	32	41	61
Medium	26	36	38	39	19	28	36	28
High	70	51	36	23	43	40	23	12
N	50	409	252	69	21	286	116	33

Source: Morris Rosenberg and Roberta G. Simmons, <u>Black and White Self-Esteem:</u>
<u>The Urban School Child</u> (American Sociological Association, 1968),
p. 144, Table 10-7.

70 percent of the black children who attributed favorable attitudes to their significant others had high self-esteem, compared to 23 percent of those who attributed unfavorable attitudes to their significant others. Among the white children, the corresponding figures were 43 percent and 12 percent. Rosenberg and Simmons conclude:

In sum, given the environments in which most of these black children currently live, many of the factors which might be expected to reduce their self-esteem—the low prestige of their race, the rejection of the black physical model, poverty, the broken family structure, and, to a lesser extent, poor school performance—do not turn out to have the anticipated consequences. The bulk of our analysis has been devoted to trying to understand why this should be so. What does have an unequivocal impact on their self-esteem in these environments is *what they believe their significant others think of them*. The great proportion of the child's daily interpersonal interactions occur with parents, friends, and teachers. If these significant others hold favorable opinions of him, respect him, and like him, then a firm foundation for healthy self-esteem may be established. Whether this foundation is sufficiently solid to withstand the buffets and assaults of adult experience is a question that our study cannot answer.[21]

CONCLUDING REMARKS

The main trends in this discussion reiterate the observation that racial attitudes, racial awareness, and racial identity are formed at an early age (about three or four) and that, for most children in the United States, the desirable color is still white. Preschool black children attach more positive and attractive qualities to white than they do to black or brown. These results were reported intitially in the late 1930s, and they continue to be reported in studies conducted as recently as 1970.

But changes are occurring in the attitudes and perceptions of black children. They are occurring mostly among black children already in school, and especially among those past the primary grades. The Rosenberg and Simmons study in Baltimore reports higher self-esteem among junior high and high school blacks than among whites. Morland reports more positive attitudes toward being black among his older black respondents than among his preschool black children. (Tables 5.16 through 5.25 appear at the end of this chapter and describe Morland's results in more detail.) Hraba and Grant report mixed results for the doll preference items and conclude that the concensus about white being better, more attractive, and more positive is beginning to crack. But studies of white children's responses made as recently as 1974 still show ethnocentric preferences.

We emphasize again, as we did at the beginning of the chapter, that all the studies referred to were conducted with white and black children who live in racially homogeneous families. None of the studies describes attitudes and identity among the unusual category of children that were the subjects of our research: the adopted black child and the white sibling in a "white" family.

In the next chapter we report these children's responses to some of the same types of instruments and tests that have been applied to more typical populations of children. The purpose of our research was not to replicate the earlier studies, because the idea of replication when the populations involved are so distinctive is foolish. But we do think it extremely useful and helpful to be able to compare the responses of our subjects with the responses of black and white children who live in typical family settings. Should our children respond in a substantially different way from that reported in most of these other studies, it would certainly be reasonable to assume that their family situation is an important factor (perhaps the crucial factor) in explaining these differences. For example, should our white subjects prove less ethnocentric in their attitudes, and should our black subjects exhibit more own-race preferences, the fact that these children are siblings must be considered important, because other conditions such as age, sex, and stimuli were not obviously altered.

TABLE 5.16 Racial preference of in-school children, by race

Racial Category of Respondents	Prefer Own Race	Prefer Other Race	Preference Not Clear
	(In Percent)		
Black (N=50)	54.0	26.0	20.0
White (N=103)	78.6	6.8	14.6

x^2 = 13.11; df = 2; p < .01

Source: J. Kenneth Morland, <u>Racial Attitudes in School Children: From Kindergarten Through High School</u>. (Final Report, Project No. 2-C-009, U. S. Department of Health, Education and Welfare, Office of Education, November 1972), p. 7, Table 4.

TABLE 5.17 Acceptance of other race by in-school children, by race

Racial Category of Respondents	Acceptance	Non-Acceptance	Rejection
	(In Percent)		
Black (N=50)	86.0	8.0	6.0
White (N=103)	66.0	15.5	18.5

x^2 = 6.94; df = 2; p < .05

Source: J. Kenneth Morland, <u>Racial Attitudes in School Children: From Kindergarten Through High School</u> (Final Report, Project No. 2-C-009 U. S. Department of Health, Education and Welfare, Office of Education, November, 1972), p. 6, Table 2.

TABLE 5.18 Responses of in-school children by race to the question, "Which child would you most rather be?"

Racial Category of Respondent	Rather Be Child of Own Race	Rather be Child of Other Race	Rather Be Neither, or Not Sure
	(In Percent)		
Black (N=50)	64.0	32.0	4.0
White (N=103)	78.6	12.6	8.7

x^2 = 8.697; df = 2; p< .02

Source: J. Kenneth Morland, <u>Racial Attitudes in School Children: From Kindergarten Through High School</u>. (Final Report, Project No. 2-C-009, U. S. Department of Health, Education and Welfare, Office of Education, November 1972), p. 9, Table 8.

TABLE 5.19 Responses of in-school children, by race, to the question, "Which man looks most like your father?"

Racial Category of Respondent	Most Like Man of Own Race	Most Like Man of Other Race	Like Neither or Not Sure
	(In Percent)		
Black (N=50)	76.0	14.0	10.0
White (N=103)	84.5	2.9	12.6

x^2 = 6.823; df = 2; p< .05

Source: J. Kenneth Morland, <u>Racial Attitudes in School Children: From Kindergarten Through High School</u>. (Final Report, Project No. 2-C-009, U. S. Department of Health, Education and Welfare, Office of Education, November 1972), p.10, Table 10.

128

TABLE 5.20 Responses of in-school children, by race, to the questions, "Which girl is the prettiest?" and "Which boy is the best looking?"

Racial Category of Respondent	Children of Own Race	Children of Other Race	Neither or Not Sure
		(In Percent)	
Black (N=50)	46.0	28.0	26.0
White (N=103)	62.1	7.8	30.1

$x^2 = 11.31$; df = 2; p<.01

Source: J. Kenneth Morland, <u>Racial Attitudes in School Children: From</u>

<u>Kindergarten Through High School</u>. (Final Report, Project

No. 2-C-009, U. S. Department of Health, Education and Welfare,

Office of Education, November 1972), p. 11, Table 13.

TABLE 5.21 Responses of in-school children, by race, to the questions, "Which girl is the best student?" and "Which boy is the best student?"

Racial Category of Respondent	Children of Own Race	Children of Other Race	Neither or Not Sure
		(In Percent)	
Black (N=50)	36.0	40.0	24.0
White (N=103)	57.3	11.6	31.1

$x^2 = 16.548$; df = 2; p<.001

Source: J. Kenneth Morland, <u>Racial Attitudes in School Children: From</u>

<u>Kindergarten Through High School</u>. (Final Report, Project

No. 2-C-009, U. S. Department of Health, Education and Welfare,

Office of Education, November 1972), p. 12, Table 14.

TABLE 5.22   Racial preferences of in-school and preschool black children

School Level	Prefer Blacks	Prefer Whites	Preference Not Clear
	(In Percent)		
In-school blacks (N=50)	54.0	26.0	20.0
Pre-school blacks (N=58)	41.4	55.2	3.4

$x^2 = 12.83$; df = 2; p $<$.01

Source: J. Kenneth Morland, <u>Racial Attitudes in School Children: From</u>

<u>Kindergarten Through High School</u>. (Final Report, Project No. 2-C-009,

U. S. Department of Health, Education and Welfare, Office of Educa-

tion, November 1972), p. 7, Table 5.

TABLE 5.23   Responses of in-school and preschool black children to the question, "Which child do you look most like?"

School Level	Most Like Black Child	Most Like White Child	Like Neither or Not Sure
	(In Percent)		
In-school blacks (N=50)	82.0	12.0	6.0
Pre-school blacks (N=58)	48.3	48.3	3.4

$x^2 = 16.25$; df = 2; p $<$ .001

Source: J. Kenneth Morland, <u>Racial Attitudes in School Children: From</u>

<u>Kindergarten Through High School</u>. (Final Report, Project No. 2-C-009,

U. S. Department of Health, Education and Welfare, Office of Educa-

tion, November 1972), p. 8, Table 7

TABLE 5.24 Responses of in-school and preschool black children to the question, "Which child would you most rather be?"

School Level	Rather Be One of the Blacks	Rather Be One of the Whites	Rather Be Neither, or Not Sure
	(In Percent)		
In-school blacks (N=50)	64.0	32.0	4.0
Pre-school blacks (N=58)	34.5	58.6	6.9

$x^2 = 9.4$; df = 2; p$<$.01

Source: J. Kenneth Morland, Racial Attitudes in School Children: From Kindergarten Through High School. (Final Report, Project No. 2-C-009, U. S. Department of Health, Education and Welfare, Office of Education, November 1972), p. 9, Table 9.

TABLE 5.25 Responses of in-school and preschool black children to the question, "Which man looks most like your father?"

School Level	Most Like One of the Blacks	Most Like One of the Whites	Like Neither or Not Sure
	(In Percent)		
In-school blacks (N=50)	76.0	14.0	10.0
Pre-school blacks (N=58)	46.5	39.7	13.8

$x^2 = 10.55$; df = 2; p$<$.01

Source: J. Kenneth Morland, Racial Attitudes in School Children: From Kindergarten Through High School. (Final Report, Project No. 2-C-009, U. S. Department of Health, Education and Welfare, Office of Education, November 1972), p. 10, Table 11.

NOTES

1. Judith D. R. Porter, *Black Child, White Child: The Development of Racial Attitudes*, Harvard University Press, Cambridge, Mass., 1971, p. 22.
2. *Ibid.*, p. 23, citing Bruno Lasker, *Race Attitudes in Children*, Holt, New York, 1929.
3. Ruth Horowitz, "Racial Aspects of Self-Identification in Nursery School Children," *Journal of Psychology*, vol. 7 (January 1939), pp. 91–99.
4. Kenneth B. Clark and Mamie P. Clark, "Racial Identification and Preference in Negro Children," in E. Maccoby, T. Newcomb, and E. Hartley, Eds., *Readings in Social Psychology*, Holt, New York, 1958.
5. H. J. Greenwald and D. B. Oppenheim, "Reported Magnitude of Self-Misidentification among Negro Children—Artifact?" *Journal of Personality and Social Psychology*, vol. 8 (1968), pp. 49–52.
6. *Ibid.*, p. 51.
7. *Ibid.*, p. 52.
8. Mary Ellen Goodman, *Race Awareness in Young Children*, Collier, New York, 1964, p. 256.
9. *Ibid.*, p. 267.
10. J. Kenneth Morland, *Racial Attitudes in School Children: From Kindergarten through High School*, U.S. Department of Health, Education, and Welfare, Office of Education, National Center for Educational Research and Development, Washington, D.C., 1972.
11. *Ibid.*, p. 24. (Emphasis added.)
12. J. Kenneth Moreland, "Race Awareness among American and Hong Kong Chinese Children," *American Journal of Sociology*, vol. 75 (November 1969), pp. 360–374.
13. *Ibid.*, p. 371.
14. Porter, *op. cit.*, footnote, p. 173.
15. J. E. Williams and J. K. Roberson, "A Method for Assessing Racial Attitudes in Preschool Children," *Education and Psychological Measurement*, vol. 27 (1967), pp. 671–689.
16. Charles E. Osgood, George J. Suci, and Percy H. Tannenbaum, *The Measurement of Meaning*, University of Illinois Press, Urbana, 1957.
17. Joseph Hraba and Geoffrey Grant, "Black Is Beautiful," *Journal of Personality and Social Psychology*, vol. 16, no. 30 (1970), pp. 398–408.
18. Morris Rosenberg and Roberta G. Simmons, *Black and White Self-Esteem: The Urban School Child*, Arnold M. and Caroline Rose Monograph Series, American Sociological Association, Washington, D.C., 1971.
19. *Ibid.*, p. 9.
20. Rosenberg and Simmons report that most of the interviewers were themselves black.
21. Rosenberg and Simmons, *op. cit.*, footnote 18, p. 144.

CHAPTER SIX

RACIAL IDENTITY AND
ATTITUDES OF TRANSRACIALLY
ADOPTED CHILDREN
AND THEIR SIBLINGS

We discussed in the previous chapter the observation that children begin to internalize a racial consciousness or identity when they are about four years old. While there appears to be more disagreement about the age at which children demonstrate racial awareness and racial preferences, the range reported by most investigators is between four and seven. White racial preferences are manifested by white, black, and Oriental children. White children identify themselves more accurately than do black children, but there seems to be evidence that black children acquire racial awareness earlier than do white children. The relationship between the respondent's race and his or her awareness, however, is not as clear as it is for the preference and identity concepts.

The focus of this chapter is to report the responses of our special children to the same stimuli described in the previous chapter, with the objective of trying to make some sense of the importance of those special circumstances.[1]

In a recent study of IQ scores among white adopted and black transracially adopted children in Minneapolis conducted by Salapatek and Weinberg, it was reported that the typical adopted child in these families, of any race, scored above the national average on standard IQ tests.

The white adopted children who found families earlier than any other group, scored 111 on the average; the black adopted children got IQ scores averaging 106, and the Asian and Indian children, who were adopted later than any other group, and more of whom had lived longer in impersonal institutions, scored at the national average, 100.

If the black adopted children had been reared by their natural parents, we would expect their IQ scores to average about 90. We infer these scores from the level of education and the occupations of their biological parents. The black and white adopted children, however, scored well above the national averages of both blacks and whites, especially if they were adopted early in life.[2]

One might hypothesize that, because there is a familial relationship among children of different races, there would be a good deal of sibling rivalry, and that a likely manifestation of sibling rivalry would be the development of more negative racial attitudes, more confusion about racial identity, and more distorted ideas of racial differences. However, familial relationships may serve to desensitize the effects that each of the above concepts usually has and thereby make the acquisition of accurate racial identity uniform across racial categories, mute the white racial preferences, and increase the likelihood that the age at which racial awareness is acquired is not affected by race.

SOCIAL CHARACTERISTICS OF CHILDREN

We think it would be helpful to provide first a brief review of the social characteristics of the children we studied. All of them lived in five cities in the Midwest. Their ages ranged from three to eight. Almost all of them had siblings who are either younger or older. Of the 366 children interviewed,

TABLE 6.1 Racial, sexual, and adoptive statuses of children subjects

Racial Background	Adoptive Status				Total
	Adopted		Born to Family		
	Boys	Girls	Boys	Girls	
White	21	21	100	67	209
Black	75	45	---	--	120
American Indian, Asian, etc.	16	21	---	--	37
Total	112	87	100	67	366

199 were adopted and 167 were born into their families. In 81 percent of the families, at least one of the children had been born to the parents.[3] Table 6.1 summarizes the racial, sexual, and adoptive status of the subjects.

RESEARCH TECHNIQUES

The procedure used for obtaining interviews with the children was to have one member of a two-person team meet with each child separately and privately. Two of the three teams of interviewers employed on the study were made up of one male and one female graduate student. Each of them took turns interviewing the parents or the children.[4] In going over the material, we found no differences between interviews conducted by men and those conducted by women. On the average, each child's interview lasted 30 minutes.[5]

INSTRUMENTS

Three separate tests or sets of materials were employed for the purpose of measuring the children's racial identity, awareness, and attitudes. The first set of materials included three baby dolls; one doll looked like a white baby, another like an American black baby of medium or dark complexion, and the third like a light-skinned black baby or an Indian or Asian baby. All dolls were dressed identically—they were clothed only in a diaper. The children were allowed to look at, hold, and play with the dolls for a few minutes while the interviewer arranged the equipment. Then the three dolls were put on the floor or on a table, and the formal interview began. The interviewer asked the child to point to the doll that:

1. You like to play with the best
2. Is a nice doll
3. Looks bad
4. Is a nice color
5. Looks like a colored child
6. Looks like a black child
7. Looks like a white child
8. Looks like you

Following these items, a second set of dolls was introduced.[6] The second set differed from the first in that three of the dolls were boy dolls and three were girl dolls. The three boy dolls were dressed identically. They were supposed to represent boys between about six and eight years old. The girl dolls were also dressed identically and represented girls within the same age range. The skin shades were the same as those of the baby dolls. The girl subjects were exposed to the girl dolls and the boy subjects to the boy dolls.

The main reason for introducing these older sex-typed dolls was to increase the likelihood that we were offering meaningful and affective stimuli for the older children in the sample. Even with the inclusion of the "older" dolls, there remained the possibility that boys who were seven and eight years old would find the dolls of little interest and that questions about which ones they would like to play with best, or were nice, or looked bad might evoke random responses. We thought, however, that we could improve the chances of obtaining meaningful responses from the older children, especially the boys, if the dolls looked like children their own age. The same eight questions were asked about the boy and girl dolls that were asked about the baby dolls.

Following the questions about the dolls, the children were shown 24 sets of pictures, each of which was pasted on a six-by-eight piece of cardboard. This instrument was adopted from the Williams and Roberson study cited in the previous chapter. Each set contained two pictures of the same object (animals, toys, umbrellas, airplanes, etc.), but colored differently. In half of the sets, one of the objects was white and the other black. The other 12 sets were dummies, and the pictures were colored red, green, blue, or orange— any color except black or white. A two-line story was attached to each set of pictures, and each story ended with the interviewer asking the children to choose the object that was *bad*, *dirty*, or *pretty*. The adjectives were adopted from the evaluation scales developed by Charles Osgood et al. and reported in *The Measurement of Meaning*.[7] The full set of adjectives is: pretty, mean, clean, bad, nice, stupid, smart, naughty, good, dirty, kind, ugly. These items provided another measure of the childrens' racial attitudes.

In the third task each child was asked to arrange and identify family members from puzzles constructed especially for the study. Fifteen figures were cut out of plywood, and each of five figures was described to the children as representing different family roles that could be fitted into five molds cut from a common plywood board. There were three mother figures, identical in size, in shape, and in the clothing painted on them. The only difference was that one had skin resembling that of a white person, another had skin resembling that of a black person, and a third had skin resembling that of an American Indian or someone from Korea, China, and so on. There were three fathers, three sisters, and six brothers (two of which had the same skin color) whose color matched that of the three mothers. The children's task was to arrange a family with five people in it and to identify the figures that looked like their mother, their father, their sister(s), or their brother(s). They were also asked to arrange families of four people and then to select a friend from one of the remaining figures. They were asked to choose which child looked most like them and with which little girl or boy they would most like to play. The children's responses to the various tasks connected with the puzzles provided measures of racial awareness, racial attitudes, and racial identity.

FINDINGS: DOLLS

The first set of results describes the children's responses to the dolls. Remember that in previous studies reported in Chapter 5 we found that white, black, and other nonwhite children tended to exhibit white racial preferences. These results were reported first by the Clarks in the late 1930s, and then by Goodman, Greenwald and Oppenheim, Moreland, and Porter.[8]

On the racial awareness and identity dimensions there was not as much consensus. The most common pattern indicated that black children are more aware of racial differences, but that white children identify themselves more accurately than do black children. Since the concept of identity includes affect, as well as cognition, and since black children are more ambivalent about their skin color, these results do not appear to be inconsistent.

The major hypothesis in this study was that the atypical environment in which the children were being reared should affect their responses in such a manner as to mute the typical white preferences and reduce differences in responses about awareness and identity that are attributable to race. Spefically, we expected that both the nonwhite and the white children would not have as strong a preference for white as had been reported for other white and black children, that the nonwhite children would not have a greater sense of racial awareness than the white children, and that the white children's racial identity would not be any more accurate than that of the nonwhites. For each dimension then, we anticipated that the nature of the children's family setting would have a sufficiently strong impact so as to alter the pattern of responses away from those most often cited.

RESPONSES TO THE DOLLS

Each respondent received a score based on the number of times he or she attributed a *positive* quality to the white doll. A child received one point each time he or she selected the white doll in response to, Which doll would you: (a) like to play with the best? (b) think is a nice doll? (c) think is a nice color? and (d) did *not* select the white doll as the doll that looked bad. Each respondent could have a score that ranged from zero to four. The *higher* the score the more times the respondent indicated a preference for the white doll by selecting it.

Table 6.2 summarizes the racial preference scores by the children's racial and adoptive status.

The scores shown demonstrate that none of the children manifested a white racial preference. Out of a possible score of four, which would have meant that the white doll was selected in response to each question, the average score was 1.7. Such a score means that none of the children selected the white dolls even half of the time. All three categories manifested the same choice patterns.

We also divided the children into homogeneous age categories and

TABLE 6.2 Mean preference scores for white baby dolls, by race and adoptive status[a]

White Children Adopted and Born to White Families[b]	Black Children Adopted	Indian-Asian Children Adopted
1.6	1.8	1.7
(153)	(101)	(43)

a Sixty-nine respondents, practically all of whom were boys older than six, did not answer all of the items that were needed to compile the score. Their partial responses were not included.

b The scores of the adopted white children were combined with those of the non-adopted white children after they were examined separately and no differences were found between the two categories.

compared racial preference scores by age as well as race. We found that the ages of the children within each racial category did not make a significant difference in their preferences (Table 6.3).

The sex of the children also did not prove to be a significant differentiating characteristic. Among the white children, the mean score for the boys was 1.6, and for the girls 1.7. Among the black children the boys' and girls' mean scores were both 1.7. Among the Indian or Asian children the boys' mean score was 1.9 and the girls' 1.6.

The children's responses were also divided, according to the interviewer's perception of the shade of the subject's skin color, into light, medium, and dark. Practically all the children described as having light skin by the interviewers were Caucasians. The children whom the interviewers described as having medium skin were black and Indian or Asian; and the children whom the interviewers described as dark-skinned were almost all black. The racial preference scores by light, medium, and dark, skin shades are summarized in Table 6.4.

Skin shade did not affect preferences for white or nonwhite dolls to a significant extent. On the whole, the mean scores of the light children were

TABLE 6.3 Mean preference scores for white baby dolls, by age, race, and adoptive status

White Children					Black Children					Indian-Asian Children				
(Ages)					(Ages)					(Ages)				
3	4	5	6	7	3	4	5	6	7	3	4	5	6	7
(22)	(37)	(32)	(25)	(39)	(18)	(28)	(9)	(8)	(7)	(12)	(11)	(4)	(4)	(12)
1.7	1.3	1.5	2.0	2.1	1.7	2.0	1.9	1.8	1.4	2.6	1.2	1.0	.8	1.8

not noticeably different than those of the medium and dark children: 1.8, 1.8, and 1.9, respectively.

. In the one skin shade category in which the frequencies were large enough to make comparisons among racial groups, the preference scores were the same for the black and Indian or Asian children of medium skin shade. Thus the light, medium, and dark children all responded to white dolls with about the same degree of positiveness. The white dolls were not given a preferential or more desirable status than the nonwhite dolls by any category of respondents.

To summarize, the children's responses to the racial preference items using baby dolls as stimuli show no bias in favor of white. Neither on the

TABLE 6.4 Mean preference scores for white baby dolls, by perceived skin shade and racial status

LIGHT			MEDIUM			DARK		
White	Black	Indian-Asian	White	Black	Indian-Asian	White	Black	Indian-Asian
(149)	(12)	(4)	(2)	(58)	(30)	(2)	(30)	(3)
(1.7)	(2.3)	(---)	(---)	(1.8)	(1.8)	(---)	(2.0)	(---)
Combined Light:		1.8	Combined Medium:		1.8	Combined Dark:		1.9
	(165)			(90)				(35)

TABLE 6.5 Mean preference scores for white boy and girl dolls, by race and adoptive status[a]

White Children Adopted and Born to White Families	Black Children Adopted	Indian-Asian Children Adopted
1.7	2.1	2.1
(185)	(115)	(37)

[a]The higher N's reflect the smaller number of answers because many more of the older children responded to these items when the older dolls were used.

basis of race alone, race and age, race and sex, or race and skin shade did any of the children exhibit white racial preferences.

The children's responses to the same four items when the stimuli were boy and girl dolls followed much the same pattern. The racial preference scores showed no significant difference between white and nonwhite children, and none of the groups exhibited a preference for the white dolls (Table 6.5).

On the whole, neither age, sex, or skin shade made a significant difference in the preference scores for the boy and girl dolls. The older Indian and Asian children (five through seven) exhibited less of a preference for the white dolls than did the younger children in that racial category. But aside from that, there were no differences by racial categories. Tables 6.6 through 6.8 provide documentation of those differences.

TABLE 6.6 Mean preference scores for boy and girl dolls, by age and race

White Age					Black Age					Indian-Asian Age				
3	4	5	6	7	3	4	5	6	7	3	4	5	6	7
1.9	1.6	1.5	1.7	1.9	2.0	2.0	2.4	2.3	1.8	2.4	2.3	1.4	1.2	1.2

TABLE 6.7 Mean preference scores for boy and girl dolls, by sex and race

| White | | Black | | Indian-Asian | |
Boys	Girls	Boys	Girls	Boys	Girls
1.7	1.8	2.0	2.0	2.0	2.1

TABLE 6.8 Mean preference scores for boy and girl dolls, by skin shades

Light	Medium	Dark
1.8	2.0	2.1
(206)	(105)	(37)

RACIAL AWARENESS

The next set of comparisons measured racial awareness, that is, the children's ability to classify the dolls into appropriate racial categories. Table 6.9 describes the percentage of children in each racial category who correctly identified the baby dolls that look like a colored child, a black child, and a white child, and Table 6.10 reports the same comparison for the boy and girl dolls. The similarity of percentages across racial categories shows that in only one instance (Table 6.10) did one group of children make more accurate identifications than did any other. The white children were more likely to identify the white dolls correctly than were the black, Indian, and Asian children.

Additional analysis however, revealed that practically all the mistakes in identification were made by children who were less than five years old, for both the baby and boy or girl dolls. (See Tables 6.11 and 6.12.)

Even among the younger-than-five children, incorrect identifications were distributed randomly across racial categories. The three- and four-year-old black children provided no more accurate identifications than the three- and four-year-old white children did.

TABLE 6.9 Percentage making correct racial identification of baby dolls, by race and adoptive status

Correct Identification	White Children		Black Children		Indian-Asian Children	
	(Percentage Making Correct Identification)					
White doll*	82	(161)	72	(105)	76	(35)
Colored doll: Lighter	43		45		52	
Darker	47	(165)	44	(107)	48	(33)
Negro doll: Lighter	33		39		43	
Darker	56	(170)	43	(108)	46	(33)

*$x^2 = 2.83$, df = 2, p<.05

TABLE 6.10 Percentage making correct racial identification of boy and girl dolls, by race and adoptive status

Correct Identification	White Children	Black Children	Indian-Asian Children
	(Percentage Making Correct Identification)		
White doll*	85	68	58
Colored doll: Lighter	41	41	28
Darker	50	43	49
Negro doll Lighter	28	30	49
Darker	60	57	30

*$x^2 = 17.8$; df = 2; p<.01

TABLE 6.11 Percentage making correct racial identification of baby dolls, by age and race

Correct Identification	White Children					Black Children					Indian-Asian Children				
Age	3	4	5	6	7	3	4	5	6	7	3	4	5	6	7
White Doll*	55	70	90	100	100	67	65	67	100	88	50	73	80	100	92
Colored doll:															
Lighter	37	44	56	52	24	36	44	33	25	38	50	73	100	50	8
Darker	47	33	41	48	76	49	37	56	75	62	33	27	0	50	92
Negro doll:															
Lighter	21	17	30	36	48	50	29	33	25	38	50	36	50	25	55
Darker	47	55	67	59	48	30	46	56	75	62	50	46	50	75	36

*x^2 4 df. = 6.3; $p<.05$

The sex of the respondents did not significantly differentiate accuracy of identification for either the baby or the boy and girl dolls, save for the black girls' more accurate identification of the baby dolls. (See Tables 6.13 and 6.14.)

RACIAL IDENTITY

On the identity dimension, the selection of the doll that looked most like the respondent, 76 percent of the white children selected the white baby doll,

TABLE 6.12 Percentage making correct identification of boy and girl dolls, by age and race

Correct Identification	White Children					Black Children					Indian-Asian Children				
Age	3	4	5	6	7	3	4	5	6	7	3	4	5	6	7
White doll*	55	65	91	90	100	45	66	100	100	92	70	36	67	100	93
Colored doll:															
Lighter	32	43	42	55	29	38	34	45	42	54	30	27	22	40	36
Darker	52	37	48	42	71	36	49	55	58	46	50	46	56	40	64
Negro doll:															
Lighter	25	23	42	23	35	23	38	46	25	23	30	46	45	20	36
Darker	35	47	55	74	65	52	55	36	75	77	40	18	33	60	57

*x^2 4 df. = 12.9; $p<.01$

TABLE 6.13 Percentage making correct racial identification of baby dolls, by sex and race

Correct Identification	White Children		Black Children		Indian–Asian Children	
	Boys	Girls	Boys	Girls	Boys	Girls
White doll*	76	89	61	86	82	72
Colored doll:						
Lighter	37	49	41	50	55	50
Darker	50	44	42	45	44	50
Negro doll:						
Lighter	33	33	39	40	36	47
Darker	57	55	39	51	55	41

*Sex differences on white doll identification: For blacks: $x^2 = 7.38, df = 1, p < .01$

Other differences not significant at $p = .05$

TABLE 6.14 Percentage making correct identification of boy and girl dolls, by sex and race

Correct Identification	White Children		Black Children		Indian–Asian Children	
	Boys	Girls	Boys	Girls	Boys	Girls
White doll*	82	87	67	69	64	52
Colored doll:						
Lighter	41	40	33	52	21	32
Darker	50	50	46	38	70	32
Negro doll:						
Lighter	25	30	29	29	50	51
Darker	60	60	60	50	29	36

*Sex differences in white identification: None significant at $p = .05$

76 percent of the black children selected either the lighter or the darker brown doll (31 and 45 percent, respectively), and 59 percent of the Indian and Asian children selected the lighter- or darker-skinned doll (21 and 38 percent, respectively). The largest proportion of children in the last-mentioned category identified themselves with the white doll (41 percent), and the smallest proportion identified themselves with the lighter-skinned brown doll, the doll that objectively bore the greatest resemblance to them. The major difference then was between the Indian and Asian children and the white and black children. But the fact that the Indian and Asian children had the lowest percentages of correct self-identifications probably results less from their ambivalence or self-rejection than from our failure to provide them with an appropriate model with which to identify.

On the whole, more accurate self-identifications were made by the older children in each racial category. (See Table 6.15.) Sex did not significantly affect the accuracy of identifications. (See Table 6.16.)

The skin shades of the respondents closely matched the skin shades of the dolls they identified as looking like them. As the percentages in Table 6.17 indicate, 62 percent of the light-skinned children selected the white baby; 60 percent of the medium children selected the lighter and darker colored dolls. Seventy-two percent of the dark-skinned children selected the two colored dolls.

The identifications of the boy and girl dolls followed a similar pattern. The older the child the more accurate the identification irrespective of race, and white and black girls made more correct self-identifications than did boys. The respondents' skin shades matched the identity choices for the boy and girl dolls even more closely than they did for the baby dolls. (See Table 6.18.)

TABLE 6.15 Correct self-identification, by age and race of baby dolls

	White					Black					Indian–Asian				
Ages	3	4	5	6	7	3	4	5	6	7	3	4	5	6	7
	60	74	90	86	90	Lighter					Lighter				
						24	33	22	25	75	25	–	25	25	55
						Darker					Darker				
						46	44	67	50	25	42	64	25	50	18

TABLE 6.16 Correct self-identification, by sex and race of baby dolls

White		Black		Indian–Asian	
Boys	Girls	Boys	Girls	Boys	Girls
		Lighter		Lighter	
71	81	31	32	10	28
		Darker		Darker	
		45	44	45	33

TABLE 6.17 Percentage making correct self-identification of baby dolls, by skin shade

Light	Medium	Dark
62 (White)	31 Lighter	36 Lighter
	29 Darker	36 Darker

TABLE 6.18 Percentage making correct self-identification of boy and girl dolls, by skin shade

Light	Medium	Dark
78 (White)	28 (Lighter)	16 (Lighter)
	42 (Darker)	64 (Darker)

SUMMARY OF RESPONSES TO DOLLS

On the basis of all the responses to the items in which dolls were used to measure racial attitudes, awareness, and identity, we found no consistent differences among the three racial categories. There was no consistent preference for the white doll among the black, white, and Indian or Oriental children. There was no indication that the black children had acquired racial awareness earlier than the white children, and there was no evidence that the white children were able to identify themselves more accurately than the nonwhite children. This is the first study of racial attitudes and identity among young children in American society that has reported no white racial preferences. Our results, then, suggest that the unusual family environment in which these children are being reared may result in their acquiring deviant racial attitudes and in their not sharing with other American children a sense that white is preferable to other races. But the children's responses also demonstrate that their deviant racial attitudes have not affected their ability to identify themselves accurately.

One could compare the responses of the black children in our study with the responses obtained by Kenneth and Mamie Clark about 30 years ago. But, aside from the obvious fact that our black respondents are being reared in white middle-class homes, so much has happened that has affected race relations in American society that such comparisons would be ludicrous even if our black children were not living under special circumstances. However, the responses in the study conducted in 1968 in Lincoln, Nebraska, by Grant and Hraba, may be compared with those given by the black children in our sample.[9] Table 6.19 shows this comparison.

The major difference between the two sets of responses is that the black

TABLE 6.19 Percentage of children preferring white doll

Request for Dolls	Hraba-Grant		Simon	
	Black Children (89)	White Children (71)	Black Children (120)	White Children (209)
Play with best	30	83	41	54
Nice doll	46	70	43	40
Locks bad	61	34	14	21
Nice color	31	48	31	49

and white children in our study responded so similarly and the black and white children in the Hraba and Grant study responded so differently, except for item 4 in which both sets of responses are almost identical. For the first two items, "play with best" and "is a nice doll," the Hraba and Grant white respondents were much more biased in favor of the white doll than were our white respondents. And on the third item, "looks bad," the black respondents in the Hraba and Grant study were much more biased against the white doll than were our black respondents. Thus comparisons between the two studies indicate greater similarity in racial preferences among our respondents than among black and white children reared in more typical environments.

PICTURES

The next group of tests examined the children's responses to the 12 sets of black and white pictures. The six negative adjectives that could be used to characterize the black and white pictures were: bad, stupid, naughty, dirty, mean, and ugly. The six positive adjectives were pretty, smart, good, clean, nice, and kind. Each subject received two scores ranging from zero to six on the basis of the number of times he or she attributed a *positive* adjective to either the black or white picture, and the number of times he or she attributed a *negative* to either the black or white picture.

For example, if a respondent associated five of the positive adjectives with white pictures and one with a black picture, he or she received a score of five on the "white" positive dimension and a score of one on the "black" positive dimension. Similarly, if he or she associated three negative adjectives with white pictures and three with black pictures, he or she received a score of three on the "white" negative dimension and a score of three on the "black" negative dimension. Table 6.20 summarizes the scores by race and adoptive status.

Note two facts about the information in Table 6.20. First, there are no significant differences in scores among the three racial categories and, second, irrespective of their own racial designation, the children were more likely to identify white objects with positive adjectives and black objects with negative adjectives. Unlike the doll situation, then, in this context, we found that children in each of the racial groupings exhibited a pro-white bias.

TABLE 6.20   Mean positive and negative scores for black and white pictures, by race and adoptive status

Black and White Picture Scores	White Children	Black Children	Indian-Asian Children
Positive			
Black pictures	2.1	2.3	2.2
White pictures	3.9	3.7	3.8
Total	6.0	6.0	6.0
Negative			
Black pictures	4.1	3.8	4.3
White pictures	1.9	2.2	1.7
Total	6.0	6.0	6.0

Dividing the children according to the interviewer's perception of their skin shade into light, medium, and dark did not significantly alter the response pattern described above. The dark-skinned children, all of whom were black, did not evaluate white and black objects differently than the medium-skinned children, most of whom were black (Table 6.21).

The children's responses were also divided into homogeneous age categories. Only among the black children did age affect scores. The older black children were more likely to associate black pictures with _positive_ adjectives and white pictures with _negative_ adjectives than were the younger children. Scores for the white, black, and Indian or Asian children within homogeneous age categories are shown in Table 6.22.

The six- and seven-year-old black children expressed more positive attitudes toward the black images than did younger children of the same race. More positive attitudes toward black images on the part of older black children are consistent with the findings of Rosenberg and Simmons.[10] They found that black high school students had higher self-esteem than white high

TABLE 6.21 Mean positive and negative scores for black and white pictures, by skin shade

Black and White Picture Scores	Light	Medium	Dark
Positive			
Black pictures	2.1	2.3	2.3
White pictures	3.9	3.7	3.7
Total	6.0	6.0	6.0
Negative			
Black pictures	4.2	3.8	3.9
White pictures	1.8	2.2	2.1
Total	6.0	6.0	6.0

school students did and that older black youths had higher self-esteem than younger blacks. They attributed the higher self-esteem to the influence of the civil rights movement and to the slogan "black is beautiful."

On the whole we did not find that the black children in our study evaluated the black images more positively than the white ones. Like their white and Indian or Asian siblings, they had higher positive scores for the white images and higher negative scores for the black images. The fact, however, that the seven- and eight-year-old black children in our sample (they represented the oldest age category) divided their positive and negative scores almost evenly between black and white suggests that by the time they are teenagers they may evaluate black images more positively than white images.

Sex made a difference only among the white children. White girls evaluated black images more positively than did white boys; and white girls evaluated black images less negatively than did white boys. White boys were the most positive in their evaluation of white images (Table 6.23).

Finally, we compared the responses of our white subjects to those re-

TABLE 6.22 Mean positive and negative scores for black and white pictures, by age and race

Black and white Picture scores	White Children (age)				
	3	4	5	6	7
Positive Scores					
Black pictures	2.1	1.3	1.7	2.2	2.7
White pictures	3.9	4.7	4.3	3.8	3.3
Negative Scores					
Black pictures	3.9	4.8	4.3	4.4	3.5
White pictures	2.1	1.2	1.7	1.6	2.5
	Black Children (age)				
	3	4	5	6	7
Positive Scores					
Black pictures	1.9	1.5	2.1	2.4	3.1
White pictures	4.1	4.5	3.9	3.6	2.9
Nagative Scores					
Black pictures	3.9	4.1	4.2	3.7	2.8
White pictures	2.1	1.9	1.8	2.3	3.2

ported by the children in the Williams and Roberson study discussed in the previous chapter.[11] The two sets of data are summarized in Table 6.24. The results show that, for 10 out of the 12 items, white children reared with black or other nonwhite siblings responded differently from white children reared in typical environments. A higher proportion of the children in the Williams and Roberson study associated white with positive and black with negative attributes than did the white children in our study. The only two adjectives for which there were no significant differences were "clean" and "dirty."

TABLE 6.22 continued

	Indian-Asian Children (ages)				
	3	4	5	6	7
Positive Scores					
Black pictures	1.9	1.6	2.1	3.0	2.4
White pictures	4.1	4.4	3.9	3.0	3.6
Negative Scores					
Black pictures	4.4	4.6	4.7	4.2	3.9
White pictures	1.6	1.4	1.3	1.8	2.1

The age ranges of the children involved in the two studies were very similar. The children in the Williams and Roberson study (1967) were between three and seven; ours were between three and eight. One might argue that geography can explain most of the differences. White children in Chapel Hill, North Carolina, are more likely to express "southern," and therefore more antiblack, attitudes than would a random selection of white

TABLE 6.23 Mean positive and negative scores for black and white pictures, by sex and race

Black and White Picture Scores	Girls			Boys		
	White	Black	Indian-Asian	White	Black	Indian-Asian
Positive Scores						
Black pictures	2.6	2.4	2.1	1.8	2.1	2.2
White pictures	3.4	3.6	3.0	4.2	3.9	3.8
Negative Scores						
Black pictures	3.7	3.8	3.4	4.4	3.9	4.2
White pictures	2.3	2.2	1.6	1.6	2.1	1.8

TABLE 6.24 Percentage of white children who attribute positive and negative adjectives to black and white pictures in two studies

Adjectives	SIMON		WILLIAMS-ROBERSON	
	White object	Black object	White object	Black object
	(189)		(111)	
	(In Percent)			
Pretty	70	30	87	13
Clean	82	17	85	15
Nice	58	42	84	16
Smart	59	41	82	18
Good	59	41	81	19
Kind	58	42	76	24
Ugly	37	63	17	83
Dirty	12	88	16	84
Naughty	31	69	8	82
Stupid	46	43	18	82
Bad	33	67	15	85
Mean	33	67	10	90

children from Illinois, Minnesota, or Wisconsin. Therefore it is the difference in geography rather than in family patterns that is the major explanation. We cannot prove the weakness of such an argument because we do not have responses from typical white children living in Illinois, Wisconsin, Michigan, and so on. But from all the data we have seen on racial attitudes in all regions of the country, we doubt that children in North Carolina, especially those who live in a university community, are likely to express opinions that are more pro-white than are children in the Midwest.

On the basis of the results of these two experiments, it appears that children reared in the special atmosphere of biracial or multiracial families have different responses to stimuli concerning race than do American children reared in typical environments. The tensions usually associated with sibling rivalry seem not to have sufficiently negative effects as to result in negative attitudes toward the race or races of their siblings. Families who have adopted transracially seem to have succeeded in providing their young children with perspectives and attitudes toward color, and presumably race, different from those held by children reared in more typical family settings. Fewer of the white, as well as the nonwhite children, in transracial homes associate the term "white" with the positive, attractive, and desirable characteristics attributed to it by white as well as black children in the rest of American society.

PUZZLES

The third set of tasks each child was asked to perform involved putting together and taking apart puzzles constructed especially for the study. A child was given three puzzles, each containing five figures which they were told were a mother, a father, two sons, and a daughter. The figures in each group of five were all painted the same shade: white, dark brown, or yellowish-brown. All the mothers, for example, were the same size and had the same clothes painted on them; similarly with the fathers, brothers, and so on. The only difference between the three mothers, and so on, was the shade of their skin.

The children were asked to perform several tasks with the puzzles. The first task was to arrange one family composed of five members. In doing so the children could select five figures of the same skin shade, or five figures of different shades. It turned out that over two-thirds of all the children, those who were themselves white, black, or Indian, arranged a family made up of persons of different skin shades.[12] They put together families with white mothers, brown fathers (or the reverse) and with brown or white children.

The pieces were then scattered, and the children were asked to put together a family that represented their family. In response, 77 and 74 percent of the white children picked the white mother and father figures; but only 48 and 56 percent of the black children and 55 and 53 percent of the Indian or Asian children selected the white mother and father figures. In fact, of course, all the children have white parents. Nevertheless, about half of

TABLE 6.25 Percentage selecting light mother and father figures, by race and adoptive status

Puzzle Selections	White Children	Black Children	Indian-Asian Children
Your Mother	77	48	55
Your Father	74	56	53

both the black and Indian or Asian children selected parental figures whose skin shades matched more closely their own. (See Table 6.25.)

The same choice pattern repeated itself when the children's responses were divided into the light, medium, and dark skin shade categories. The medium and dark children were much less likely to select the light mother and father than were the light-skinned children. (See Table 6.26.)

Neither age nor sex had any effect on the children's selections. Younger black and Indian or Asian children were as likely as older children in these categories to select the skin shades that matched their own. Boys' selections were similar to those of girls.

The parent figures were removed, and the subjects were next asked to choose from among three sets of nine children's figures those figures that looked like them and like their brother(s) and sister(s). The children's choices are described in Table 6.27.

TABLE 6.26 Percentage selecting light mother and father figures, by skin shade

Puzzle Selections	Light Skin	Medium Skin	Dark Skin
Your Mother	75	50	48
Your Father	76	55	46

On self-identity, 71 percent of the white boys and 61 percent of the white girls selected the white figure, and 78 and 76 percent of the black children selected the dark or the medium-brown figure.

Among the Indian or Asian children, 58 percent of the boys and 59 percent of the girls selected the medium and dark figure, but a large minority selected the lightest of the children figures. The Indian or Asian children, like the white and black children, identified themselves correctly in the matching of the sex of the figures with their own. We do not believe that the selection of the light figures by 40 percent of the Indian or Asian children should be attributed to errors of cognition. Rather, we are more inclined to believe that, just as the dolls did not provide good enough models for these

TABLE 6.27 Self- and sibling selections, by sex and race

Puzzle Selections	White		Black		Indian-Asian	
	Boys	Girls	Boys	Girls	Boys	Girls
	(In Percent)					
Self						
Light	71	61	21	14	42	41
Medium	17	26	31	35	42	35
Dark	12	13	47	41	16	24
Brother						
Light	36	43	51	50	38	14
Medium	29	32	20	18	25	50
Dark	35	25	29	32	37	36
Sister						
Light	53	44	53	32	33	50
Medium	21	28	23	48	42	20
Dark	26	28	24	20	25	30

children, the puzzle pieces also were not appropriate enough stimuli. They failed to provide the children with appropriate figures with which to identify.

The figures in Table 6.27 show that, unlike the selection of parental figures, the choices of brothers and sisters were not biased in favor of any racial category. There was no tendency for white children to overselect whites, or for blacks to over- or underselect blacks. The children's selections were most probably based on their real-life situations, since we know that 83 percent of the nonwhite children have at least one white sibling and that all the white children have at least one nonwhite sibling.

The final set of tasks involving the puzzle figures asked the children to select the boy and the girl they would most like to play with, and then the boy and the girl they would most like to have visit them. These choices are described in Table 6.28. Race appears not to be a prominent concern in the children's selection of friends. There is no indication from the percentages in Table 6.28 that white children overselected white figures or that black children overselected figures whose skin colors were closest to their own. Nor did they overselect white figures. The friendship choices, like the sibling choices, seem unaffected by color.

When the responses were compared by skin shade, there was also no systematic preference for either light- or dark-skinned children. (See Table 6.29.)

Sex probably would have been an important predictor of friendship choices, but the task confronting the children was to select *the boy and the girl* with whom they would like to play and visit, and therefore the children did not have to make a choice on the basis of sex.

CONCLUDING COMMENT

To summarize the results of the various experiments described in this chapter, it appears that black children reared in the special setting of multiracial families do not acquire the ambivalence toward their own race reported in all other studies involving young black children. Our results also show that white children do not consistently prefer white to other groups, and that there are no significant differences in the racial attitudes of any of the categories of children. Our findings do not offer any evidence that black children reared by white parents acquire a preference for black over white. They show only that black children perceive themselves as black as accurately as white children perceive themselves as white. It is still too early to say whether this sense of black identity will persist, and what affect will be attached to it as these children grow up.

TABLE 6.28 Friendship selections, by sex and race

Puzzle Selections	White		Black		Indian-Asian	
	Boys	Girls	Boys	Girls	Boys	Girls
	(In Percent)					
Girl play						
Light	44	28	66	44	33	22
Medium	39	37	27	17	34	22
Dark	17	35	7	39	33	56
Boy play						
Light	33	48	39	16	45	33
Medium	33	23	29	52	33	33
Dark	34	29	32	32	22	34
Girl visit						
Light	38	40	47	38	50	50
Medium	31	50	23	31	25	25
Dark	31	30	30	31	25	24
Boy visit						
Light	44	30	43	21	55	31
Medium	34	43	26	41	18	54
Dark	32	27	31	38	27	15

On the matter of identity, we found no evidence that white children made more accurate designations than black children. So again on this dimension, these findings depart from the mode. The Indian and Asian children had lower scores, but it is much more likely that their scores are an artifact of poor equipment and faulty design than a measure of their sense of identity.

There was only one instance in which the black children showed less awareness, or perhaps ambivalence, regarding their identity than did the

TABLE 6.29 Friendship selections, by skin shade and sex

Puzzle Selections	Light Boys	Light Girls	Medium Boys	Medium Girls	Dark Boys	Dark Girls
			(In Percent)			
Girl play						
Light	42	27	50	33	83	60
Medium	42	37	36	26	-	-
Dark	17	35	14	41	17	33
Boy play						
Light	37	41	41	27	8	33
Medium	30	25	32	47	46	42
Dark	34	34	27	27	46	25
Girl visit						
Light	37	36	50	50	43	60
Medium	29	29	20	29	43	20
Dark	34	36	30	21	14	20
Boy visit						
Light	47	27	43	25	42	31
Medium	22	45	31	54	16	23
Dark	32	29	26	21	42	46

white children, and that was in the matter of selecting puzzle figures with skin shades that matched those of their own parents. The blacks, as well as the Indian or Asian children erred more than the white children in selecting figures whose skin shades matched their own rather than the figures whose skin shades more closely resembled those of their parents. They did not make this error in selecting figures that represented either themselves or their siblings.

As indicated in Chapter 5, most previous studies of young children's racial preferences have reported pro-white attitudes on the part of white, black, and Indian or Oriental children living in the United States. Other studies have suggested that black children acquired an awareness of race earlier than white children but were less likely accurately to identify themselves as black. In other words, while black children are able to discriminate between racial categories at an earlier age than white children, because the concept of identity involves feelings or affect about race, black children's responses are likely to be less accurate than white children's. The less accurate scores for identity measures are consistent then with the greater ambivalence black children manifest in their attitudes toward race. While some of the studies referred to go back two or three decades, even those made in the 1960s, the era when slogans such as "black power" and "black is beautiful" became popular, young black children continued to exhibit pro-white attitudes.

It appears on the basis of the findings reported in this chapter that the practice of transracial adoption is having a significant, perhaps even a revolutionary, impact on the racial identity and attitudes of young black and white children. However, it is still too early to predict with any degree of accuracy what is likely to happen to these children in later years, during their adolescence and adulthood. It may be that the attitudes and prevailing tones of the larger society will have sufficient impact so as to alter or confuse the identity and attitudes formed within the relatively unique setting of these multiracial families.

NOTES

1. The black children in our study differ also because almost all of them lived in professional, middle-class families in white neighborhoods.
2. Sandra Scarr-Salapatek and Richard A. Weinberg, "The War over Race and IQ: When Black Children Grow Up in White Homes," *Psychology Today*, vol. 9, no. 7 (December 1975), p. 81.
3. In total there were 708 children in the 204 families; but only 366 fell within the appropriate age range.
4. All the interviewers were white.
5. A tape recorder was in operation during the entire period the interviewer and child were together. But the child's responses were also recorded on an interview schedule. The main purpose for recording the interviews was to pick up any additional impromptu reactions the child might have, for example, comments the subject might make about the research, about his or her older or younger siblings, and about having been adopted. Having the interviews on tape also provided some measure of the child's affect, whether or not the child manifested hostility or anger during the interview, whether he or she was apathetic, whether the subject sounded confused or tentative. Permission to record the interview was

obtained initially from each parent. The manner in which the machine worked was demonstrated to each child at the outset of the interview.

6. The choice of dolls and the questions were adapted from the work of the Clarks reported in the previous chapter: Kenneth B. Clark and Mamie P. Clark, "Racial Identification and Preference in Negro Children," in E. Maccoby, T. Newcomb, and E. Hartley Eds., *Readings in Social Psychology*, Holt, New York, 1958. The questions are exactly as phrased by the Clarks; we wanted to be able to compare the responses of our subjects with the responses obtained by the Clarks or with any other studies that had been made using these items.

7. Charles E. Osgood, George J. Suci, and Percy H. Tannenbaum, *The Measurement of Meaning*, University of Illinois Press, Urbana, 1957.

8. The specific references to these studies are cited in Chapter 5.

9. Joseph Hraba and Geoffrey Grant, "Black Is Beautiful," *Journal of Personality and Social Psychology*, vol. 16, no. 30 (1970), pp. 398–408.

10. Morris Rosenberg and Roberta G. Simmons, *Black and White Self-Esteem: The Urban School Child*, Arnold M. and Caroline Rose Monograph Series, American Sociological Association, Washington, D.C., 1971.

11. J. E. Williams and J. K. Roberson, "A Method for Assessing Racial Attitudes in Preschool Children," *Education and Psychological Measurement*, vol. 27 (1967), pp. 671–689.

12. Sixty-eight percent of the white children, 85 percent of the black children, and 80 percent of the Indian or Asian children arranged "mixed" families.

SECTION THREE

ALTERNATIVES TO
TRANSRACIAL ADOPTION

The chapters in this section on subsidized adoption and single-parent adoption are included because we think it is useful to describe the major alternative types of adoption of nonwhite children that have been and are being considered by adoption agencies throughout the country, and because implicitly the comparison must be between these forms of adoption and transracial adoption as to which is the most viable method for emptying institutions of hard-to-place children.

It is not our intention, in describing these alternative mechanisms, to urge a choice on the reader. The results of the empirical study reported in Section Two describe feelings and reactions of parents to their status as adoptive parents of nonwhite children and the racial and social identity and attitudes of the adopted nonwhite children and their white siblings. These findings demonstrate that, at least during childhood, blacks and whites can live

together as brothers and sisters, perceive each other as they are—
different—and yet respect and love each other for their differences as well as
for their sameness. Our data do not permit conclusions as to whether these
responses can continue in adolescence and adulthood. Neither of course do
the data in Section Two speak to the larger sociopolitical issues involved
when white adults act as the major socializing agent for black children.

Both Sections One and Three discuss these issues. Section Three describes
two of the more prevalent alternatives to transracial adoption that do speak
directly to the sociopolitical issues involved in the socializing and controlling of thousands of black children.

CHAPTER SEVEN

SUBSIDIZED ADOPTION

Would transracial adoption have gained the support and momentum it did, albeit briefly, if the supply of white adoptable children had not diminished, and/or if adoption agencies had made more concerted efforts to recruit and support nonwhite families? The answer to both these questions is "no." Even many of the strongest proponents of transracial adoption believe that, were it not for the two factors mentioned above, transracial adoption would not have been the placement of choice for nonwhite children. There have always been professionals who have argued that "marginally acceptable" nonwhite families present, in the long run, a healthier environment for nonwhite children than the more acceptable (translate "higher socioeconomic status") white families. This position in recent years has gained considerable support, and several schemes are currently underway to implement this philosophy.

Subsidized adoption, the process whereby a family legally adopts a child while the state, via an adoption agency, assumes some part of the financial obligations incurred for maintaining the child, has become one of the most workable and appealing of the alternatives to transracial adoption. Although the practice is still too recent for much literature to have accumulated on it, this chapter is devoted to a review of the material available.

Subsidized adoption rests on the assumption that adoption is in the best interests of almost every parentless child. Although not a new development, it signifies a fundamental shift in adoption ideology away from the position that, after the adoption is final there is no further formal agency involvement with the adoptive parents, to the position that the agency will continue to maintain an ongoing monetary relationship with the adoptive parents. But the child, nevertheless, is the legal responsibility of the adoptive parents.

In most cases after a subsidized adoption arrangement has been made final, statutes do not require the agency to serve in a monitoring capacity; nor do the majority of agencies attach any casework obligations to their financial contributions. The adoptive parents may, for a limited period after the adoption is formalized, voluntarily attend meetings or group sessions devoted to discussing common experiences, but in most instances the continuance of subsidies is not contingent on the parents' attendance at these sessions.

As an alternative to any other type of adoptive procedure, subsidized adoption has been endorsed by the CWLA. The league's 1973 SAS states:

Provision should be made for supplementing the income of families that have the essential qualifications required to meet the needs of adopted children but that are unable to assume financial responsibility for the full cost of a child's care.

Subsidies that would make it possible for a child to have both a permanent home and continuity of care and affection are clearly a more beneficial arrangement for a child. . . . A more positive use of subsidy is expected to result in the adoption of more non-white children who might not otherwise be placed.[1]

As of August 1975, 41 states had statutes pertaining to subsidized adoption, a number that had almost doubled in less than 10 years. Although there are some differences among the states regarding subsidized-adoption legislation, each state has recognized that the subsidies must be arranged prior to an adoption being made and that the subsidies are intended to be supplemental in nature. In no instance are the subsidies designed to provide for a child's total financial support.

In a majority of statutes, subsidized adoption payments are specifically linked to the state's foster care scale. The wording of Maryland's 1975 law and Illinois's 1969 statute, are typical of other state's legislation. Maryland law calls for:

A monthly payment may not exceed 75 percent of the regular care rate of the foster care rates for board and clothing. . . . This subsidy shall be continued on a monthly basis for as long as necessary, subject to annual redetermination of the child's needs and the family's continued request for a subsidy.

Illinois states that:

The Department may provide financial assistance, and shall establish rules and regulations concerning such assistance, to persons who adopt physically or mentally handicapped, older and other hard-to-place children who immediately prior to their adoption were legal wards of the Department. The amount of assistance may vary, depending upon the needs of the child and the adoptive parents, but must be less than the monthly cost of care of the child in a foster home. Special purpose grants are allowed where the child requires a special service but such costs may not exceed the amounts which similar services would cost the Department if it were to provide or secure them as guardian of the child.[2]

However, if pending amendments to Maryland's subsidized-adoption law were to be enacted, subsidies would be made equal to the costs involved for foster care, as indicated by the amendments' wording:

Subsidies and services for children under this program shall be provided out of funds appropriated to the Department for the maintenance of children in foster care or made available to it from other sources. . . .[3]

The subsidy may be either for special services only or for money payments, and either for a limited period or for a long term. The amount of the limited or long-term subsidy may not exceed . . . the allowable amount for a child under foster care. . . .[4]

In 1969, California enacted the Dymally Adoptions Bill. This bill is a variation of subsidized adoption, because payments are limited to a maximum of five years, and monthly grants are not to exceed the foster care payments scale. It has already played an important role in aiding in the adoption of hard-to-place (e.g., nonwhite) children by their foster parents. For example, in 1973–1974, 388 of 836 adoptions were consummated as a result of this bill, many of them inracial black adoptions.[5]

Opinions differ as to whether or not adoption subsidies should be tied to the financial requirements of the adoptive families (e.g., a means test) or to the specific needs of the child (e.g., education, medical). This matter is usually resolved in favor of the child's needs, as can be seen by the following excerpt from a pending amendment to Maryland's subsidized-adoption law.

This payment is designed to cover a specific expense involved with the particular adoption of a child or children. It could include:

A. Legal costs connected with the adoption
B. Costs of particular medical services or equipment which could not be met through any other resource such as medical assistance, crippled children's service, etc.
C. Cost of a particular service (physical or psychiatric)
D. Other costs related to the adoption of a specific child by a particular family which would be a severe strain on the family's finances[6]

If additional amendments were to be included in Maryland's present law, however, categorical subsidy would be redefined as follows: "The subsidy will vary with the needs of the child due to his *special circumstances* as well as the availability of other resources to meet the child's needs. . . ."[7] In a previous section of the law, special circumstances are defined as:

1. Physical or mental disability
2. Emotional disturbance
3. Recognized high risk of physical or mental disease
4. Age
5. Sibling relationship
6. Racial or ethnic factors; or
7. Any combination of these special circumstances.[8]

Practically every statute has the proviso that subsidies are to be granted for the purpose of having a parentless child adopted by an otherwise eligible family only after other nonsubsidized avenues have been exhausted. This condition appears to be the overriding one under which the majority of subsidies are granted. In effect then, subsidized adoption is seen as a method of last resort, reserved specifically for the adoption of hard-to-place children who otherwise would not be placed in an adoptive home.

Although the regulations of individual states vary, most deal in some manner with such issues as: (1) the subsidy's duration (short or long periods) but usually not to be enforced once the child reaches his or her eighteenth birthday and in some states the twenty-first; (2) the amount of the subsidy (tied in some fashion to foster care payments); (3) the method of payment: categorical allocations marked for direct payments such as medical, special education, or direct grants, or when applicable, payments attached to public assistance; (4) income limitation of adoptive families; and (5) periodic reexamination of financial eligibility.

The above requirements are incorporated in the 1975 Model State Subsidized Adoption Act developed by the CWLA for the Children's Bureau of the Office of Child Development.

In most cases, the conditions under which eligibility for a subsidy is determined relate to whether the child falls into one of the hard-to-place categories. One of the characteristics of hard-to-place is nonwhite. Most subsidized-adoption laws recognize race as a criterion determining whether a subsidy should be used in order to increase a child's eligibility for adoption. Maryland, in fact, includes race as a special circumstance under which subsidies can be awarded. It may be argued therefore that subsidized adoption is of particular benefit to nonwhite children, for they constitute one of the largest blocs within the hard-to-place definition.[9] A reasonable conclusion, then, to the widespread use of subsidies to prospective nonwhite adoptors of nonwhite children would be a reduction in the number of nonwhite children available for adoption and consequently a curtailment of transracial adoption.

In support of the cost-effectiveness hypothesis of adoption and its variants over foster care or institutional placement is an August 1975 report entitled, *Foster Care and Adoptions: Some Key Policy Issues*, prepared for the Subcommittee on Children and Youth of the Senate Committee on Labor and Public Welfare. The report notes that, in 1971, of the approximate 330,373 children in foster care (as compared with 241,900 in 1960), 69,943 (21 percent) were either in institutions or group homes. It argues that institutional placement is the most expensive type of nonadoptive care (i.e., more than double that of foster care). Of note is the fact that approximately 100,000 children in foster care in 1971 were legally eligible for adoption, and 90 percent of these children were classified as children with special needs (i.e., hard to place). The report, in a direct statement of fact, clearly argues the merits of adoption over nonadoptive placements:

It is a simple but impressive calculation to sum up the savings that would result from moving to adoptive homes only one-half of the 100,000 children in foster care who are available to be freed for adoption. In making that calculation, it is important to remember the number of years that each of the children would stay in foster care unless special efforts were made. For example, it is estimated that the cost of care for a single infant who entered the New York foster care system in 1971 will amount to $122,500 by the time the child reaches 18 years of age.[10]

Some contend that the popularity of subsidized adoption represents a major refocusing by adoption agencies away from their traditional function of supplying childless couples with children to that of finding adoptive families for parentless children.[11] Such interpretation may be correct if one assumes that "benevolence" is the major factor motivating the adoption agencies. But two different factors may also be operating. First, subsidized adoption is more cost-effective (less expensive) than other types of long-range programs,[12] and therefore more attractive to budget-minded agencies. For example, since practically all subsidized-adoption payments are in some manner linked to a state's foster care schedule, even though the subsidies may equal the maximum allowable amount paid to foster parents for the temporary care of parentless children, the state would save money; it would avoid the risk of a child's being moved from foster parent to foster parent, moves which increase overall costs to the state for agency time spent in effecting such transfers. This is in addition to the crucial fact that subsidized adoption is adoption, and that the benefits that accrue to both parent and child are immeasurable.

When one considers the expense of subsidized adoption compared to the expense of maintaining a child in an institution, the former is also clearly less expensive to the state. Table 7.1 compares Maryland's 1974 schedule of payments for both individual foster families and institutions. Note that when an individual foster family (or subsidized adoption) provides a home for a twelve-year-old child requiring special care, the costs are still considerably less than the lowest rate for group care.

States that have begun to implement limited subsidized-adoption programs report significant financial savings over other types of nonadoptive practices (e.g., foster care). For example, in September 1975, Michigan reported that, during the first half of 1974, 130 subsidized adoptions were made, costing the state $63,692.67. Were these children to have remained in foster care, the cost to the state for the same period would have been $150,115. Thus Michigan realized a savings of $86,422, or 57 percent.[13]

In addition, both Ohio and Illinois describe similar savings using subsidized adoption in lieu of foster care. Over a two-year period, Ohio reported a cost benefit for 36 children of $20,547, and Illinois, projecting until the age of 18 the costs of 45 children adopted under subsidy who would have otherwise remained in foster care, realized a savings of

$292,518.[14] Thus, not only does subsidized adoption appear to reduce significantly a state's financial burden, it also allows both parent and child to "normalize" their relationship into one more acceptable to all. The state's financial responsibilities could be reduced further if pending legislation introduced by Senator Alan Cranston were to be enacted by Congress. Senator Cranston's bill (S1593, Opportunities for Adoption Act of 1975), which proposes a program somewhat similar to the Aid to Families with Dependent Children Program, would have the federal government reimburse the states for subsidized-adoption programs. Furthermore, a program of adoption would allow many more nonwhite families to adopt. That subsidies would increase the available number of couples considering adoption can be strongly inferred from J. L. Simon's analysis of the relationship between the number of foster homes and the level of payments. Using a regression analysis, Simon cross-sectionally examined by year the data from 32 states including the District of Columbia and concluded "that there is indeed a positive relationship between the level of foster-child payments and the number of foster homes offered and that the size of the relationship is fairly substantial—an elasticity of perhaps 0.50–1.0. This suggests that doubling the foster-child payment level would increase the number of foster homes offered by 50 to 100 percent."[15]

Sufficient evidence exists to support the argument that many foster parents would adopt their foster children were it not for their own limited finances.[16] In fact, some state laws regarding subsidies stipulate, and many imply, that payments should be awarded only to foster families who wish to adopt children originally placed in their care, where a relationship has already been demonstrated.[17] Apparently this is the assurance sought by many legislators that public money is being well spent.[18] For example, Missouri's subsidized-adoption law calls for foster parents with whom a child has lived for 18 months to have "preference and first consideration" should the child be placed for adoption.[19] Massachusetts law clearly indicates that "any person in whose home such child has been placed by the division shall also be informed by the department if such child has become eligible for adoption, and such person may request consideration as a prospective adoptive parent."[20] Under the title "Procedure for Obtaining Approval for a Subsidized Adoptive Agreement," Maryland law strongly suggests that foster parents be given preference in the adoption of their foster children: "Whenever it appears that a child under public or voluntary agency care, legally free and in need of adoptive placement should be adopted only by foster parents with whom emotional ties have been established . . . an

TABLE 7.1 Board rates and monthly clothing allowances for foster care of children

Foster F·mily Care Under Local Departments: The following rates are paid
for each foster child cared for by a family which is under the direct
uspervision of the local department of social services.

Kind of Care	Board		Monthly Clothing Allowance	Total Board and Clothing Allowance
	Monthly	Per Diem		
Regular Care				
Infant through age 5	$70.00	$2.35	$11.00[a]	$ 81.00
Age 6 through age 11	71.00	2.35	17.00[a]	88.00
Age 12 and older	83.00	2.75	21.00[a]	104.00
Special Care				
Infant through age 5	98.00	3.25	11.00[a]	109.00
Age 6 through age 11	98.00	3.25	17.00[a]	115.00
Age 12 and older	98.00	3.25	21.00[a]	119.00
Emergency Care				
(All ages)	90.00[b]	3.00[b]	NONE[c]	90.00

Purchase of Care from Institutions and Agencies: The following rates
apply to the foster child who is cared for through an institution or
agency. The local department supervision of the foster child is
through the institution or agency. Payment is made for actual costs
for each foster child not to exceed the maximums indicated in this
schedule.

Kind of Care	Board and Clothing Allowance Actual up to:	
	Monthly	Per Diem
Individual Foster Family Care	$225.00[c]	$ 7.50[c]
Group Care (Institutions or Group Homes)		
Low Rate	275.00 d	8.35
Intermediate Rate	600.00 d	19.15
High Rate	700.00 d	22.50

[a]To cover purchase and upkeep of clothing, personal care and school
supplies. Also eligible for initial clothing allowance per Schedule C.
If an initial clothing allowance is granted in a particular month, the
monthly clothing allowance will not be paid for that month.

[b]An additional amount may be set by local policy to provide payment to
hold space available or a higher rate or both, not to exceed $125.00
per month per child including any payment for holding space available.

[c]Eligible for initial clothing allowance, but ineligible for monthly
clothing allowance.

[d]Includes $25.00 clothing allowance.

Source: State of Maryland Employment and Social Services, 7.02.11,

Schedule B, B1, p. 105

application may be made to the social services administration to certify the child as eligible for subsidy."[21]

There appears to be a consensus that subsidies should not be used as an incentive to adopt, but that its availability should be made known to potential adoptive parents as part of the informational package.[22]

A not insignificant side benefit of increasing the number of available nonwhite adoptors is that it would satisfy and comply with some of the demands of those who are opposed to transracial adoption by providing agencies with a much greater pool of potential nonwhite adoptive families to draw on, and at the same time accomplish a reduction in some of the agencies' rigid eligibility criteria. While subsidies should not be defined as a "money-making" enterprise, it may be that the subsidy can be used in a recruitment campaign as a legitimate incentive to persuade a nonwhite family to adopt. Precedent for this type of "fee-for-service" program already exists within foster care, where foster parents receive sums compensating them for the responsibilities and attention required by children with special needs, in addition to compensation for actual expenses.[23] In addition, as early as 1964, Pennsylvania initiated a successful quasi-adoption program aimed at increasing the inracial adoption of black children. The subsidies offered to black parents who otherwise might not have adopted resulted in the legal adoption of many of these children.[24]

All the above considerations are germane to the topic of the ultimate adoption of nonwhite children. In 1967 it was estimated that in Los Angeles and New York the percentage of nonwhite children either in foster care or institutionalized (i.e., hard to place) ranged from 50 to 80 percent, respectively, and these children represented only about 8 percent of the adoptions in both cities. The well-established negative relationship between the length of time a child spends in a nonfamilial environment and the chances of eventual adoption clearly indicates that for a majority of these children adoption under conventional conditions would not be forthcoming.[25] Thus, in states where subsidized adoption is allowable it appears both desirable and logical to link hard-to-place children with potential foster and adoptive parents willing to adopt but financially unable to do so. An added benefit to this linkage would be to systematically account for all children in other than adoptive long-term placements. A much needed "goodness-of-fit" safety valve would have to be added in order to guard against the chance that children would be "lost in the system" and spend their childhood in temporary placements devoid of family life.

Save for the important introduction of subsidies into the business of bringing together prospective adoptors and available, yet unadoptable, children, the procedures just described are in fact the basic functions of ARENA. ARENA is a system instituted in 1967 whereby cooperating states and agencies can determine through computerized data which children are in placement, why they are there, and what plans are being developed for them which will shorten the length of time they spend in a nonfamilial setting. Since its beginning ARENA has successfully placed 1410 hard-to-place children in various parts of the United States. At the end of 1974, 1094 children were awaiting placement, and 1577 potential adoptive families were awaiting children. These figures result from referrals made by about 827 registered agencies. The family/child ratio is somewhat misleading, since many families had stated certain preferences regarding the children they would accept. For example, although there were 626 children between the ages of 7 and 12, only 495 families stated that they were willing to accept children between these years.[26]

It is important to note that the term "hard-to-place" appears to be shifting away from racial minorities to children with physical and emotional handicaps. In fact, ARENA no longer places American Indian children in the hard-to-place category and reports that a third of the families registered with them specify their preference for American Indian children.[27]

ARENA, however, does not confine itself to the placement of nonwhite children but seeks to place permanently all categories of hard-to-place children. Nor are agencies affiliated with ARENA usually geographically bound to place a child within their own state's jurisdiction. For example, if a potential adoptive family in the Northeast is particularly suited to care for a hard-to-place child from the Southwest, an arrangement can be made facilitating the child's interstate transfer. However, because of the lack of uniformity in the statutes of the various states, interstate placement of children is at times difficult to achieve.[28]

ARENA could prove to be a particularly useful vehicle for serving as an alternative to transracial adoption if agencies could locate a pool of prospective black adoptive families (race being one descriptive variable noted on a child's or family's computer profile) eligible on all levels but the financial one. The strengths of a family could be linked with the needs of a child, and a subsidy offered to consummate the adoption.

On the basis of 1972 data, it is estimated that approximately 21,600 nonwhite children (of which 15,100 were black) have been adopted.[29] Although overall adoptions appear to have fallen somewhat in 1972, the number of nonwhite adoptions remained fairly stable. The number of actual nonwhite adoptions in all probability belies the more accurate figure of between 40,000 and 80,000 *potentially* adoptable nonwhite children. [30] To what extent an offer of subsidy payments to prospective adoptive black parents would increase the frequency of nonwhite adoptions is difficult to predict. All that can be said on the basis of limited documentation is that the number would increase.[31]

Even though the subsidy concept has been gaining popularity, the actual number of subsidized adoptions remains quite small, hardly enough to be significant for alleviating the problem of parentless children, at least at the present time, but important as a harbinger of what is possible. For example, from January 1 to May 15, 1975, Illinois approved adoption subsidies for 1319 children,[32] compared with only 240 for the years 1969–1971.[33] Of these children, 664 were black, 1255 were over the age of two years (868 of whom were older than six years), and 330 had some type of handicap (physical, emotional, or intellecutal).[34] There is no indication that any of the subsidized adoptions were transracial.

In New York, which was the first state to pass a subsidized adoption law in September 1968, there were 302 such adoptions for January to June 1970.[35] By 1973, 1484 subsidized adoptions had occurred. When compared with the state's total number of adoptions in 1971 (11,375)[36] and 1972 (10,073)[37] the subsidized-adoption figure is small but promising.

New Jersey, during a period of 16 months beginning July 25, 1973, completed 161 subsidized adoptions of hard-to-place children, 81 of whom were black and 17 biracial (black-white). Significantly, New Jersey's definition of hard-to-place children no longer included black infants, although biracial children and all children over the age of seven were so defined.[38]

Of these 161 children, 132 were adopted by their foster parents. This figure is more important than it may appear. Foster parents who legally adopted their foster children under this subsidy plan received less financial assistance per month than they would have had the children remained with them in foster care. This weakens an old myth that foster parents are "in it for the money" and rarely adopt. In fact, the Los Angeles Department of Adoptions reports that of 539 children adopted in 1973–1974 as a result of their Reach-Out Program, 35 percent were adopted by their foster parents.[39] As compared with whites, there is no indication of the extent to which black couples in the New Jersey program adopted their foster children, nor is there any evidence pertaining to whether any of these adoptions were transracial. However, there is no reason to assume the latter.

One of the reasons it is difficult to discuss the impact of subsidies on adoption and especially on nonwhite adoption is the lack of data and the absence of a center for distributing what data are available. It appears that there is no single (federal) depository where these data, if available at all, can be found. Any meaningful analysis, then, of nationwide trends in subsidies is extremely difficult. In fact, it is not even incumbent on the individual states to generate such data, let alone furnish them to any government agency. This is also true in relation to overall adoption figures which the Department of Health, Education, and Welfare has been collecting since 1957, and particularly statistics relating to transracial adoption. For example, the preliminary figures for adoptions in 1972 published by this department in February 1975 were based on data received from 37 states. Of these 37 states, however, 7 submitted only partial data. The figures for 1971 were based on 42 reporting states, with 3 of these states submitting incomplete data.

CONCLUDING REMARKS

Although adoption in our society is, by this time, an acceptable method of achieving a nonbiological family, it by no means implies a stigma-free status. Subsidized adoption, akin in the minds of many to a public dole, increases the risks of stigmatization, both for the adoptee and the adoptive family. Not only is being an adopted child a somewhat dubious distinction, but popular thinking might be scornful that his or her adoptive parents "had to be paid" in order for him or her to achieve this status. The apparent nervousness on the part of some professionals is that subsidized adoptions will be defined by many as a variation of public assistance.[40] Underlying this issue are the positive societal values placed on individual volition and self-reliance, without which dependency, and therefore welfare payments, are a possible result.

To some, the word "subsidized" also has the negative connotation of "being paid to love," and is confused, according to this line of thinking, with "being paid not to work." This type of logic is based on a definition of morality and virtue rooted in a popular notion which dictates that people should engage in an activity not because of payment but because they have a genuine desire to do so and derive satisfaction from it. What is not accounted for by these individuals is that subsidies to potential adoptive parents cannot be conceptually separated from federal subsidies awarded to farmers and industrialists. Should not industry be held responsible for the same standards of self-sufficiency as adoption?

How then will the widespread use of subsidies to prospective nonwhite adoptors affect transracial adoptions? The answer in all probability is that it will tend to reduce their number. As an operational concept, subsidized adoption has been in effect since September 1968. It is considered by many to be an appropriate way of locating nonwhite homes for nonwhite children[41] and has successfully raised the number of inracial nonwhite adoptions. Its continued use will be advocated by those hostile to black-white adoptions as a way of reducing the already dwindling number of transracial placements. Clearly, white couples wanting to adopt a nonwhite child will be ineligible for subsidies because, as a group, they are in the higher occupational and financial brackets and are rarely, if ever, foster parents. The latter usually receive the "most favored" treatment in subsidy allocation.

But stumbling blocks exist. For example, some subsidized adoptions are experimental in design, subject to periodic evaluation and thus sensitive to the political nuances of accountability. How would the possible legislative curtailment of funds already allocated to a subsidized-adoption program affect both the adoptors and the adoptee? Could parents, especially low-income nonwhite adoptive parents, be reasonably assured that subsidies would continue on a regular basis or, should that not be possible, that alternative programs could be arranged without the taint of public assistance? If such assurance is not feasible and legislation regarding subsidies is rescinded, would potentially adoptable children be returned to agencies or, in the case of legalized adoption, once again be placed for adoption?

These questions are yet to be fully answered. As to the original query concerning the weight that subsidies to otherwise eligible nonwhite adoptive families will have on the continuance of transracial adoption, the evidence points in the direction of a significant impact. Subsidies have increased nonwhite inracial adoption[42] and made possible other adoptions previously deemed "impossible."[43] Although subsidized adoption is not a panacea for the plight of parentless nonwhite children, the fact that subsidies allow more inracial nonwhite adoptions, especially by foster parents, joined with other factors that increase the attractiveness of conventional inracial nonwhite adoption (single-parent, quasi, etc.) tends to work against the transracial adoption of black children by white couples.

NOTES

1. Child Welfare League of America, *Standards for Adoption Service*, revised, Child Welfare League of America, New York, 1973, pp. 72, 73, Section 7.5; p. 92, Section 0.8.
2. Illinois, Public Act 76-1683, approved October 6, 1969.
3. Maryland State Subsidized Adoption Act, House Bill No. 1552.
4. *Ibid.*, Section 88C, 1975; Section 88E (C,1).
5. *National Adoptalk*, vol. VIII, no. 1 (January–February 1975).
6. Maryland, 07.02.12, Section 07 D2.
7. Maryland, 88E C, Bill No. 1552, 1975. (Emphasis added.)
8. *Ibid.*, Section 88A.
9. Andrew Billingsley and Jeanne M. Giovannoni, *Children of the Storm: Black Children and American Child Welfare*, Harcourt, New York, 1972, p. 199.
10. U.S. Senate, Committee on Labor and Public Welfare, Subcommittee on Children and Youth, *Foster-Care and Adoptions: Some Key Policy Issues*, Washington, D.C., August 1975, p. 18.
11. Kenneth W. Watson, "Subsidized Adoption: A Crucial Investment," *Child Adoption*, no. 4 (1972) pp. 20–28.
12. *Ibid.*; Child Care Association of Illinois, *Subsidized Adoption: A Study of Use and Need in Four Agencies*, Child Care Association of Illinois, Springfield, Ill., 1969.
13. Report submitted to the State of Michigan, Department of Health, Education, and Welfare, Children's Bureau.
14. *Ibid.*; State of Ohio, 1973; State of Illinois, 1970.
15. Julian L. Simon, "The Effect on Foster-Care Payment Levels on the Number of Foster Children Given Homes," *Social Service Review*, vol. 49, no. 3 (September 1975), p. 410.
16. Watson, *op. cit.*, footnote 11, p. 21.
17. Angela Gentile, "Subsidized Adoption in New York: How Law Works—and Some Problems," *Child Welfare*, vol. 49, no. 10 (December 1970), pp. 576–80; Harriet L. Goldberg and Llwellyn H. Linde, "The Case for Subsidized Adoptions," *Child Welfare*, vol. 48, no. 2 (February 1969), pp. 97–99, 107; Charles Lansberry, "A Major Question in Subsidized Adoption," *Child Welfare*, vol. 47, no. 8 (October 1968), Readers Forum, pp. 499–500.
18. Ursula Gallagher, "Adoption Resources for Black Children," *Children*, vol. 18, no. 2 (March–April 1971), p. 50.
19. Missouri Stat. Ann., 453.070 (Supp. 1974).
20. Massachusetts Sess. Law, 433 (1973).
21. Maryland Subsidized Adoption Act, No. 1552, Section 88D.
22. "Utilization of Subsidies to Increase Black Adoption," Proceedings of a Conference, Chicago, October 12–14, 1971, p. 6.
23. Most foster care agencies do not salary foster parents of children with special needs, preferring instead to base their payments on a scale consisting of direct costs above the

standard rate, parental time expenditure, and level of skill required to provide adequate child care. These payments at times are as much as $350 per month above the regular monthly rate. Virginia Peterson, "Payment for Foster Care: Cost-Benefit Approach," *Social Work* (July 1974), pp. 426–431.

24. Roberta G. Andrews, "Permanent Placement of Negro Children through Quasi-Adoption," *Child Welfare*, vol. 47, no. 10 (December 1968), pp. 583–86, 613.
25. Henry A. Maas and Richard E. Engler, *Children in Need of Parents*, Columbia University Press, New York, 1959.
26. *ARENA News*, Annual Report, Child Welfare League of America, 1974.
27. Arlene L. Nash, "Reflections on Interstate Adoptions," *Children Today* (July–August 1974) pp. 7–11.
28. Roberta Hunt, *Obstacles to Interstate Adoption*, Child Welfare League of America, New York, 1972.
29. *Adoptions in 1972*, DHEW Publication No. (SRS) 75-03259 NCSS Report E-10 (1972), National Center for Social Statistics, February 1975.
30. Elizabeth Herzog, Cecelia Sudia, Jane Harwood, and Carol Newcomb, *Families for Black Children, The Search for Adoptive Parents: An Experience Survey*, HEW, Office of Child Development, Children's Bureau, Supt. of Documents, U.S. Government Printing Office, 1971, p. 67.
31. Watson, *op. cit.*, footnote 11, p. 22.
32. State of Illinois, Department of Children's and Family Services, Subsidized Adoption Data Report, May 20, 1975.
33. Subsidized Adoption Act, *op. cit.*, footnote 21.
34. Herzog et al., *op. cit.*, footnote 30.
35. Watson, *op. cit.*, footnote 11, p. 22.
36. U.S. Department of Health, Education, and Welfare, *Adoptions in 1971*, Washington, D.C., 1971, p. 7, Table 1.
37. U.S. Department of Health, Education, and Welfare, *Adoptions in 1972*, Washington, D.C., 1972, p. 5, Table 1.
38. Josephine Bonomo, "Subsidies Aid Adoption," *New York Times*, January 5, 1975, p. NJ4.
39. *National Adoptalk*, vol. 11, no. 1 (January–February 1975).
40. Watson, *op. cit.*, footnote 11, p. 25.
41. Hunt, *op. cit.*, footnote 28.
42. Mary Polk, "Maryland's Program of Subsidized Adoption," *Child Welfare*, vol. 49, no. 10 (December 1970), pp. 581–83.
43. Katherine B. Wheeler, "The Use of Adoptive Subsidies," *Child Welfare*, vol. 48, no. 9 (November 1969), pp. 557–559.

CHAPTER EIGHT

SINGLE-PARENT ADOPTION

The function of any type of adoption is to attempt to construct a mechanism resembling as closely as possible the functions and responsibilities of the nuclear family. Any type of adoption should be able to provide the structure within which a child or several children can experience the activities society allocates to the family.

In addition to subsidized adoption, several variations of and substitutes for conventional inracial two-parent adoption have been suggested. For example: quasi-adoption, permanent foster care, variations of institutionalization (e.g., group homes, collectives), and single-parent adoption. Save for the last-mentioned, the literature does not indicate any widespread use of these adoption variations significant enough to make a dent in reducing the population of parentless black children. Our guess is that, if a choice had to be made concerning workable replacements for transracial adoption, the second most promising form would be single-parent adoption.

The basic question of single-parent adoption is whether one legal parent (male or female) is better for a parentless child's development than any of the other options that do not involve parents. Viscerally the answer appears to be positive. What happens, for example, when one of the parents of any young child dies, or divorce occurs? The child remains to be reared by one parent. The latter is a natural consequence. Adoption, however, is a planned event, still somehow not quite natural, and therefore open to scrutiny and quasi-scientific examination.

Why not consider the 43 million single adults[1] in this country—one out of every three adults—as a possible pool of potential adoptive parents? Of course a substantial percentage would be ineligible either of their own volition or by society's standards. But this would still leave an unknown, presumably rather large, number of eligible individuals. Consideration by adoption authorities of the 21 million "recently single" (11.7 million widowed, 5.9 million divorced, and 3.3 million separated) adults along with the 22 million who have never married would help bolster the ranks of those individuals who could be used as resources for parentless children.[2]

"Single-parent adoption" should not be confused with "single-parent family," a term used to describe a home where one of the natural parents is absent (once referred to as a broken home). The popularity and acceptance of single-parent families, perhaps a result of changing life-styles, especially as they affect the aspirations of women, should make it easier for those involved in adoption to come to peace with the idea of defining single individuals *other than natural parents* as potential adoptors. The fact that one-seventh of all children (about 9 million under the age of 18) are being raised in approximately 4.2 million single-parent families, 35 percent by black women (up from 28 percent in 1970), should make the notion of single parents more palatable.[3] Indeed, between 1960 and 1973 there has been an increase of 67 percent in father-headed single-parent families.

Without the taint of forced treatment, adoption agencies interested in using the concept of single-parent adoption, especially with black children, could suggest cooperative projects with such organizations as Parents Without Partners and Young Single Parents to help adoptive singles in the initial stages of their parenthood. One could also argue that many of the children being raised by one parent are likely eventually to be incorporated into the traditional nuclear family as a result of the marriage of either their mother or father. There is no reason to assume that this does not also apply to single-parent adoptions.

As with any other new development, the prevalence of the single-parent concept (family or adoption) has its ripple effects in social policy. A 1975 Senate Subcommittee on Children and Youth held sessions evaluating the effects of government-financed programs on single-parent adoptions.[4] Testimony was heard on how to improve day care service and on the 9 A.M. to 5 P.M. workday, two issues of particular importance in maintaining the single-parent idea.

The single-parent adoption, like any other type of unconventional adoption, is an instrument reluctantly created by adoption agencies in their attempts to cope with the unbalanced equation between hard-to-place children and a lack of available homes. But, the labeling of these children as hard to place, or as having special needs, and the consonant nontraditional adoptive designs reserved solely for them, does them a disservice. It creates an almost impossible situation whereby most, if not all, conventional *qua* normal adoptive placements are closed to the children by dint of their categorization (i.e., stigma). It is as if the adoption agencies guaranteed that special children would be eligible only for "innovative" adoptions.

As in the case of all other nontraditional adoptive arrangements, single-parent adoptions are reserved for "residue children," those who are physically and emotionally handicapped, usually past the age of five, biracial, black, or a combination of any of the above. If one were to rank-order the desirability of nonconventional adoptive patterns, single-parent adoptions would fall beneath all other two-parent designs. In fact, most adoption agencies see single-parent adoption as appropriate only if no other two-parent situations can be arranged.[5]

In referring to the qualifications adoptive parents should have, the CWLA's SAS clearly states that "families should be selected in which a husband and a wife are living together and the marriage has been of sufficient duration to give evidence of its stability."[6] Hedging somewhat, it continues, "In exceptional circumstances, when the opportunity for adoption for a specific child might otherwise not be available, a single parent (who may be unmarried, widowed, or divorced) should be given consideration."[7]

Single-parent adoption, then, has never been considered the placement of choice, but rather one reserved for special children and turned to when other more conventional avenues of adoption did not exist.

As a serious alternative to the more common two-parent adoption, single-parent adoption started in the mid-1960s when the California Department of Social Welfare (followed afterward by New York City's Division of Adoption Service) revised its regulations and allowed single individuals to apply for adoption.[8] By 1965 the Los Angeles County Bureau of Adoptions had placed more than 30 children with single individuals.[9] At no time, however, were unmarried individuals given initial preference by adoption authorities. Singles were eligible only after a two-parent family could not be located and then were to be considered only for "leftover" (i.e., hard-to-place) children.

The two-parent nuclear family thus continues to be a generally acceptable definition of family life, and all other nonnuclear types, such as single-parent arrangements, are perceived as somehow deviant. But using children's emotional disturbance as the popular yardstick by which familial success is measured, there are data suggesting that children raised in single-parent families (for whatever reason—death, divorce, mental illness) are as mentally healthy as their counterparts who are reared with two parents.[10] Yet even though adoption agencies claim to base their policies on scientific evidence, single-parent adoptions rank quite low in their hierarchy of options for adoptable children. In fact, when single-parent adoptions are made, assurances are sought from the adoptor (usually assumed to be female) that an extended family is available so that the child will have some contact with males.[11] By itself, the idea of a child's having contact with an extended family makes good sense, especially as they can be helpful to a single parent in emergency situations such as illness. Issue is taken when the implication is that single-parent adoptive families are somehow only half as good as conventional adoptive families, and that the extended family will compensate for the absence of one parent.

Again the SAS contends that "in such cases [single-parent adoptions], it is important for the child that the single parent should be a member of a family to which the child can have the security of belonging."[12]

Where in the hierarchy single-parent adoption falls in relation to transracial adoption is an interesting question. In theory, if a white couple seeks to adopt a nonwhite child, they will receive priority over a single individual wanting to adopt, even if the latter is racially similar to the child. Whether this would in fact occur is, however, dependent on the host of contingencies previously discussed. In any event, many observers would seriously question the prevailing assumption that a two-parent family of a race different from the child's is better for a child's development in the long run than a single parent of the same race.

As with subsidized adoption and other variants of the historic two-parent inracial matched adoption, the development of single-parent adoption once enacted into law and accepted by adoption agencies increases the available pool from which potential adoptive parents can be drawn. If eligible black single individuals (of both sexes) are included in this expansion, it would further reduce the need for, and therefore use of, transracial adoption as a method of obtaining homes for black children.

NOTES

1. Jo Ann Levine, "Between Loneliness and Satisfaction," *Baltimore Sun* March 2, 1975, p. 1.
2. *Ibid.*
3. Georgia Dullea, "The Increasing Single Parent Families," *New York Times*, December 3, 1974, p. 46; "Census Cites Rise in Blacks' Status," *New York Times*, July 28, 1975, p. 9.
4. *Ibid.*; Sheila K. Johnson, "The Business in Babies," *New York Times Magazine* (August 17, 1975), p. 65.
5. Velma Jordan and William Zittle, "Early Comments on Single Parent Adoptive Homes," *Child Welfare*, vol. 45, no. 9 (November 1966), pp. 536–538.
6. Child Welfare League of America, *Standards for Adoption Service*, 1973, revised, Child Welfare League of America, New York, 1973, p. 50, Section 5.19.
7. *Ibid.*
8. Rita Kramer, "The Revolution in Our Adoption Laws," *Parents' Magazine* (December 1971), p. 37; Lois Dickert Armstrong, "One Parent is Better Than None," *Good Housekeeping* (February 1967), pp. 69, 162, 163.
9. Armstrong, *op. cit.*, footnote 8.
10. Alfred Kadushin, "Single Parent Adoption: An Overview and Some Relevant Research," *Social Service Review*, vol. 44, no. 3 (September 1970), pp. 263–274.
11. *Ibid.*; "The Family: Half a Home Is Better Than None," *Time* (December 8, 1967), pp. 44, 49.
12. Child Welfare League of America, *op. cit.*, footnote 6.

CONCLUSIONS

Transracial adoption came into being largely because as a society we place high value on the nuclear family and on its ability to develop for its members the strengths needed to cope with their future experiences. As a society, we believe that the nuclear family is a better environment for most children to be raised in than other types of settings, such as foster care, group homes, or institutions. Transracial adoption was developed as a method by which nonwhite children who seemed destined to spend their childhood and adolescent years in nonfamily contexts could be legally adopted by white parents and thereby experience family life. It was not meant to be an instant cure for thousands of homeless nonwhite children, nor was it even the placement of first choice when racially similar adoptive families were available.

Transracial adoption thus gained momentum because traditional adoption procedures, inspired by historic conditions, failed parentless nonwhite children and their respective communities. Social work agencies involved in adoption related to it in a love-hate fashion. Charges and countercharges were hurled toward society in general, but particularly at adoption agencies for causing the backlog of parentless nonwhite children by not relating realistically to the life-styles of black couples who wanted to adopt racially similar children. Adoption agencies (white-controlled) were condemned for relying on antiquated rigid eligibility policies standardized by white measures. Social work agencies reacted defensively in their efforts to defend the matching concept.

Champions and opponents of transracial adoption never minced words or attempted to couch their arguments in nuances. At times, charges of white and black (and Indian or Oriental) racism were the order of the day. The social work profession was indicted along with the courts for allowing the situation to develop, and then for working toward maintaining the status quo.

As we write in the beginning of 1976, it appears that we are witnessing the demise of transracial adoption as a significant alternative to homelessness. Some placements may still be made but, as a highly visible social movement, transracial adoption appears to be dead. This volume has documented some of the factors that led to its birth, development and expansion, and demise. The first section described the history, prevalence, and types of transracial adoption. It reviewed studies of American Indian and black children who have been placed in white families and reported the extent to which these placements were successful as measured by agreed-on standards for the child's adjustment and the parents' satisfaction.

The second section described the results of our survey of 204 families, each of whom had adopted at least one nonwhite child. The focus of our survey was on racial identity, awareness, and attitudes of the adoptive nonwhite children and their white siblings. The most significant finding that emerged from our survey was the absence of a white racial preference or bias on the part of the white and nonwhite children. Unlike other findings thus far reported for young American children, those reared in these homes appear indifferent to the advantages of being white but aware and comfortable with the racial identity that their outward appearance imposes on them. By and large the parents exude confidence that the atmosphere in which these children are being reared, the relationships, the values, and the lifestyle they are exposed to, will carry them through to successful personal adjustments as adults. Studies that should be conducted two decades hence will confirm or deny the truth of the parents' prophecy.

The last section reviewed two of the main alternatives to transracial adoption that have come to the fore as the demise of transracial adoption has become more and more apparent: subsidized adoption and single-parent adoption. It is the subsidized-adoption program that thus far appears to be the most prevalent alternative. Its appeal is primarily to those black couples who want to adopt one or more children and who meet all the criteria for adoption save the financial ones. Such families may be provided with a subsidy which varies from $80 to $120 per month. Thus far, several thousand families have been the recipients of such subsidies. The presence of the financial subsidy does not limit or change the legal status of the child vis-à-vis his or her adopted parents. Such a child is as legally and completely adopted as if there were no subsidy.

We conclude on the ironic note that institutionalized alternatives to transracial adoption are gaining support and acceptance just as studies such as the one reported in Section Two are beginning to surface which describe socialization experiences on the part of black and white children which are unique to American society. These findings indicate that transracial adoption appears to be a mechanism whereby children can develop racial "color blindness." In other words, transracial adoption appears to provide the opportunity for children to develop awareness of race, respect for physical differences imposed by race, and ease with their own racial characteristics, whatever they may be. As we have emphasized many times, and wish to do again, it is still too early to say how these children (those transracially adopted and their nonadopted siblings) will develop, whether their "color blindness" and their lack of prejudice or bias toward nonwhites will remain with them as a permanent characteristic or whether the realities of American society will cause alterations in these attitudes. It is also too early to say with whom these adopted children who belong to minority racial and ethnic groups will identify: how they will characterize themselves, with which community their ties will be closest, and how they will relate to their white parents and siblings. If the fears expressed by black and Indian opponents of transracial adoption are realized, that these children will be white on the inside and black on the outside, and that they will be perceived by both white and black as pariahs, transracial adoption will be remembered as a dismal and emotionally costly experiment. If the hopes and expectations of the parents involved in transracial adoption are realized, and their children are emotionally whole, well-adjusted, and able to move easily within and between black and white communities, society's failure to maintain and support the program will be remembered with deep regret. Time, thus, will determine transracial adoption's final evaluation.

INDEX